India

a cross-curricular theme

CURRICULUM LINKED

6393C

India *(Upper)*

Published by PrimEd Publishing® 2010
Copyright© R.I.C. Publications® 2010
ISBN 978-1-84654-225-1
PR– 6393

Titles available in this series:
India *(Lower)*
India *(Middle)*
India *(Upper)*

Internet websites

In some cases, websites or specific URLs may be recommended. While these are checked and rechecked at the time of publication, the publisher has no control over any subsequent changes which may be made to webpages. It is *strongly* recommended that the class teacher checks *all* URLs before allowing pupils to access them.

View all pages online   **Website:** www.prim-ed.com

Foreword

India (Upper) is one of three books designed to provide opportunities for pupils to discover some of the natural, physical, cultural, economic and political aspects of this fascinating and extremely diverse Asian country and its people. The books in this series give selected information about both modern and ancient India and use a wide variety of activities across many learning areas.

Contents

Teachers notes

The book has been organised into nine sections covering a variety of aspects about India:

- Geography
- Modern India
- Folktales and legends
- History
- Religions, customs and celebrations
- The arts
- Symbols
- Landmarks
- Famous people

Groups of pupil pages within each section follow one of two formats:

- a single pupil page is accompanied by a corresponding teachers page; or
- sets of three pupil pages are accompanied by a corresponding teachers page.

This provides the pupils with as many varied activities as possible.

Teachers notes pages

All teacher pages follow the same format.

Relevant **teacher information** is given, particularly background information which teachers may require about the topic or to answer pupils' questions.

Any necessary information about how to use the worksheet with the pupils is also provided.

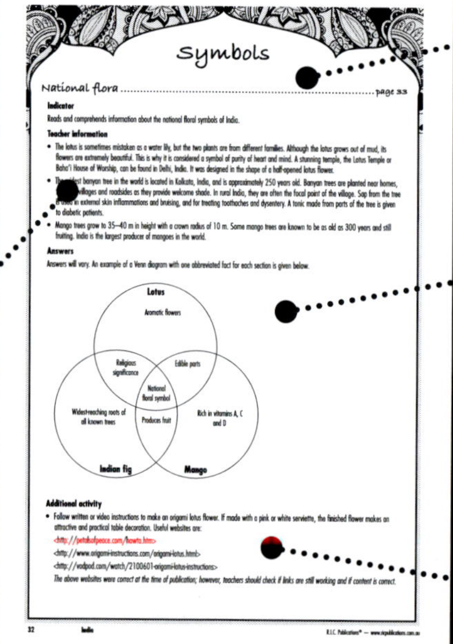

The **section**, **title** and **page number** of each corresponding pupil page is given.

Answers are provided for pupil pages where necessary.

At least one **additional activity** to support or extend the pupil activity on the worksheet are supplied. Many of these extend across other learning areas.

Pupil activity pages

All pupil pages provide information as well as an activity to complete. Sometimes the two will be combined.

Many pupil pages contain some **information** about the topic at the top. This is written in pupil-friendly language and provides information needed to complete the activity.

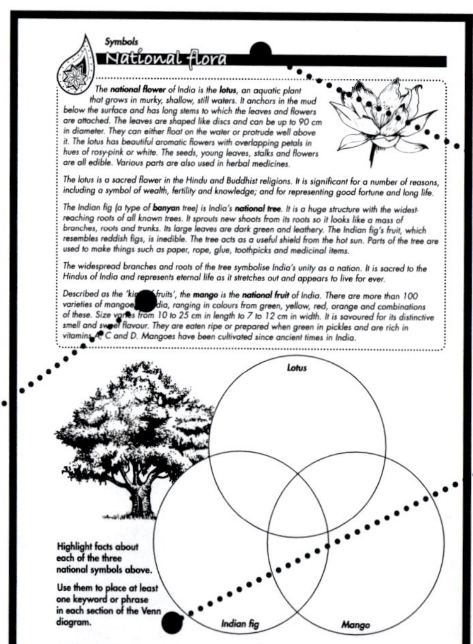

The **section and title** of each pupil page is given.

Clear, concise **instructions** for completing the pupil activity are supplied.

Curriculum links

Country	Level	Subject	Subject strand	Objective
England	Key Stage Two (Years 5 and 6)	English	Reading	• use inference and deduction and look for meaning beyond the literal • use print and ICT-based reference and information material
			Writing	• write for different purposes and audiences • write in a range of forms
		Mathematics	Number	• use number operations to solve problems
			Handling data	• represent and interpret data using graphs and diagrams
		History		• know about the social, cultural, religious and ethnic diversity of societies studied in wider world • know about historical events and changes • study a past society; e.g. the Indus Valley
		Geography		• use maps • identify and describe what places are like and where they are • describe and explain how places are similar and different to other places in the world • study a locality that is less economically-developed
		Religious education		• describe the key aspects of religions, especially stories and traditions
		Art and design		• design and make images and artefacts • know about artists from different cultures
Northern Ireland	Key Stage Two	Language and literacy	Reading	• justify their responses logically, by inference, deduction and reference to evidence within the text
			Writing	• write for various purposes and audiences
		Mathematics and numeracy	Number	• use operations to solve problems
			Handling data	• interpret tables and diagrams
		The world around us		• know how we are interdependent with the wider world for some of our goods and services • compare people and places; for example, lifestyles, housing, transport and education • study the effects of a lack of basic resources on a place and people's lives • study the effect of extreme weather conditions in the world

				• know about the impact of inventors and inventions over time • know about the traditions of other cultures • study the life of a famous person from the past
		The arts	Art and design	• look at and talk about the work of artists from other cultures and use their appreciation to engage in art making
		Personal development and mutual understanding		• develop an awareness of the experiences, lives and cultures of people in the wider world • appreciate the range of cultures and traditions in other countries
Republic of Ireland	5th and 6th Class	English language	Reading	• engage with an increasing range of text • use comprehension skills • read and interpret different kinds of functional text
			Writing	• experience interesting and relevant writing challenges • write in a wide variety of genres
		Mathematics	Number	• solve problems involving whole numbers and simple percentages
			Data	• represent and interpret data using pie charts
		SESE	History	• know about people who have made a contribution to the lives of people in other countries • discover myths and legends from different cultural, ethnic and religious backgrounds • relate myths and legends to the beliefs and traditions of the peoples from which they came • explore common themes and features in myths and legends • study the peoples of the Indus valley
			Geography	• develop understanding of the names and location of major natural and human features of the world • engage in practical use of maps • study the lives of people in a location in another part of the world • become aware of the ethnic, religious and linguistic groups of people in the world • become aware of the characteristics of some major climatic regions in different parts of the world
		Arts education	Visual arts	• look at and talk about the work of artists

   India

Scotland	Second	Literacy and English	Reading	• respond to literal, inferential and evaluative questions and other close reading tasks
			Writing	• explore different genres and use what learn to create own texts
		Numeracy and mathematics	Number, money and measure	• solve problems, including percentage-related problems
			Information handling	• interpret and display data
		Social studies	People, past events and societies	• know why people and events from a particular time in the past were important
			People, place and environment	• study a contrasting area to Britain and investigate the main features of weather and climate and their impact on living things • interpret information from maps and locate key features in the wider world
			People in society, economy and business	• discuss diversity of cultures and customs • look at lifestyles of citizens in another country
		Expressive arts	Art and design	• be inspired by a range of stimuli to express own ideas through art and design • respond to the work of artists by discussing thoughts and feelings
		Religious and moral education	World religions	• investigate and reflect upon stories of world religions • explain key features of festivals and celebrations • describe practices and traditions of world religions
Wales	Key Stage Two	English	Reading	• read in different ways for different purposes • experience a wide range of texts
			Writing	• write for a range of purposes and in a range of forms
		Mathematics	Skills	• solve problems
			Handling data	• use and present data, in tables and charts
		Geography		• identify and locate places using maps • study life in a country with a different level of economic development to the United Kingdom
		History		• identify significant people and why they did things
		Art and design		• examine the methods used by other artists and craftworkers from other cultures and places

Geography

Objective

Uses a map to gain geographical information about India.

Teacher information

- India is an independent nation made up of 28 states and seven union territories. It is part of the Eurasian landmass and covers a land area of 2 973 193 km². Two of India's neighbours, Bangladesh and Pakistan, were once part of India. East and West Pakistan became independent of India, in 1947 (separated in the middle by India); then in 1971, East Pakistan became independent of West Pakistan and became known as Bangladesh.

- India (sharing with Nepal) boasts the third highest mountain in the world as part of the Himalayas. Mount Kanchenjunga rises 8586 m above sea level. The Ganges River (the Ganga), considered one of the most significant rivers in the world, runs a 2510 km course from the Himalayas to the Bay of Bengal.

- Calcutta (Kolkata) was the original capital city of India until 1911, when the British decided to move India's capital. New Delhi became the official capital of India in 1947. As well as being a city, it is located within the National Capital Territory of Delhi. New Delhi is home to the offices of federal government and the Parliament of India.

Additional activity

- Use an atlas to record the longitude and latitude of each capital city pupils located on the map and listed in the table on page 4.

Answers

Pages 3–4

1. Teacher check

2. (a) Afghanistan, Pakistan, Nepal, China, Bhutan, Bangladesh, Myanmar
   (b) Arabian Sea, Indian Ocean, Bay of Bengal
   (c) Thiruvananthapuram and Srinagar

3. See table below

State	Capital	State	Capital
Andhra Pradesh	Hyderabad	Maharashtra	Mumbai
Arunachal Pradesh	Itanagar	Manipur	Imphal
Assam	Dispur	Meghalaya	Shillong
Bihar	Patna	Mizoram	Aizawl
Chhattisgarh	Raipur	Nagaland	Kohima
Goa	Panaji	Orissa	Bhubaneshwar
Gujarat	Gandhinagar	Punjab	Chandigarh
Haryana	Chandigarh	Rajasthan	Jaipur
Himachal Pradesh	Shimla	Sikkim	Gangtok
Jammu and Kashmir	Srinagar (summer), Jammu (winter)	Tamil Nadu	Chennai
Jharkhand	Ranchi	Tripura	Agartala
Karnataka	Bangalore	Uttarakhand	Dehradun
Kerala	Thiruvananthapuram	Uttar Pradesh	Lucknow
Madhya Pradesh	Bhopal	West Bengal	Kolkata
Union territory	**Capital**	**Union territory**	**Capital**
Andaman and Nicobar Islands	Port Blair	National Capital Territory of Delhi	Delhi
Chandigarh	—	Lakshadweep	Kavaratti
Dadra and Nagar Haveli	Silvassa	Puducherry	Puducherry
Daman and Diu	Daman		

Page 5

4. Chandigarh is the capital of two states (Punjab and Haryana). It is also a Union Territory.

5. Important geographical features — rivers, mountains, deserts, plateaux etc.

6. (a) Thar Desert   (b) Ganges River   (c) New Delhi
   (d) Vindhya Mountain Range   (e) Tropic of Cancer
   (f) Bay of Bengal

7. (a) northern India   (b) southern India   (c) northern India
   (d) northern India   (e) southern India   (f) northern India

Map of India – 1

1. **Look carefully at the map of India. It shows the states and union territories together with each one's capital city.**

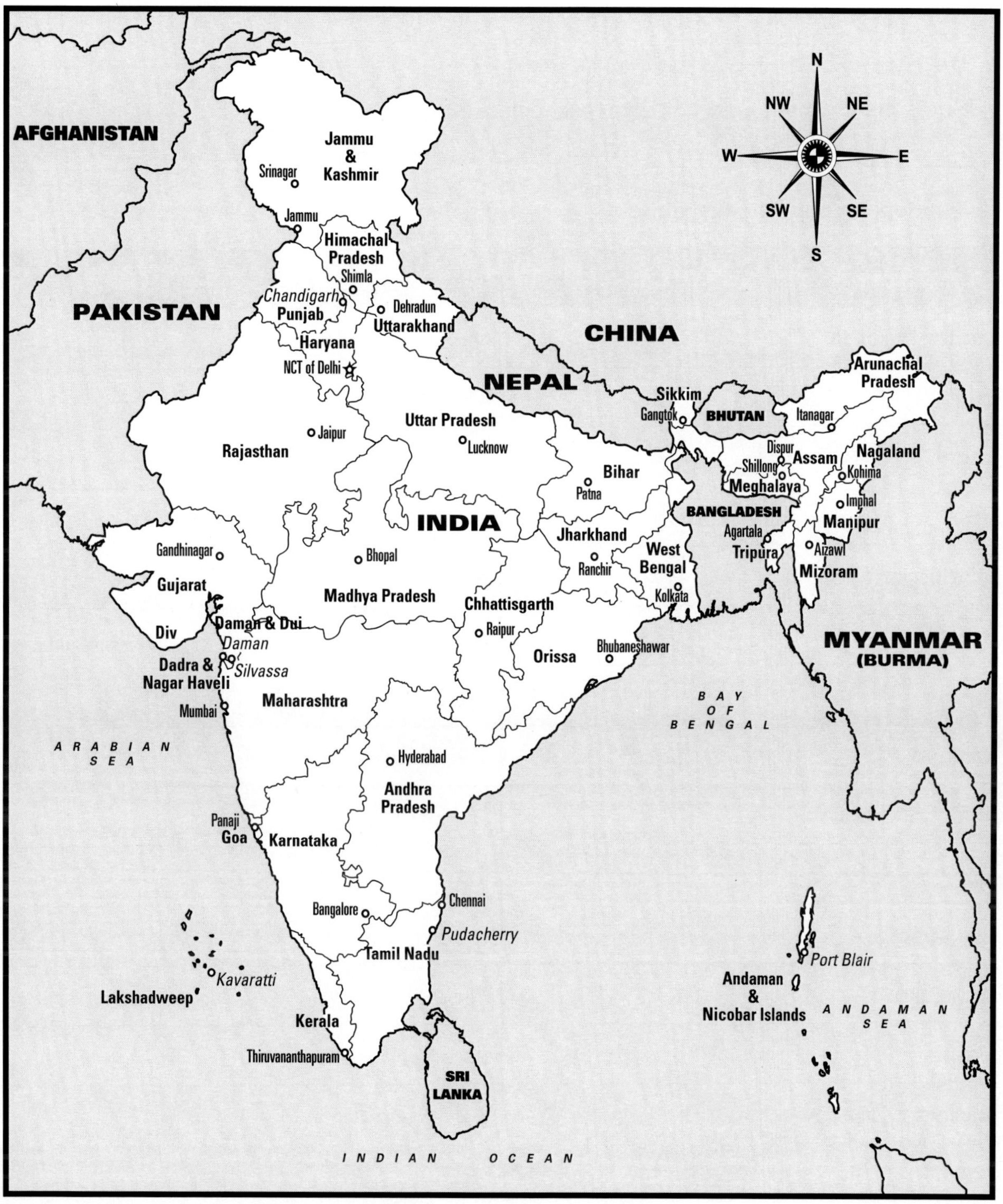

2. **Use the map to complete these questions.**

(a) Name the seven countries which share a border with India.

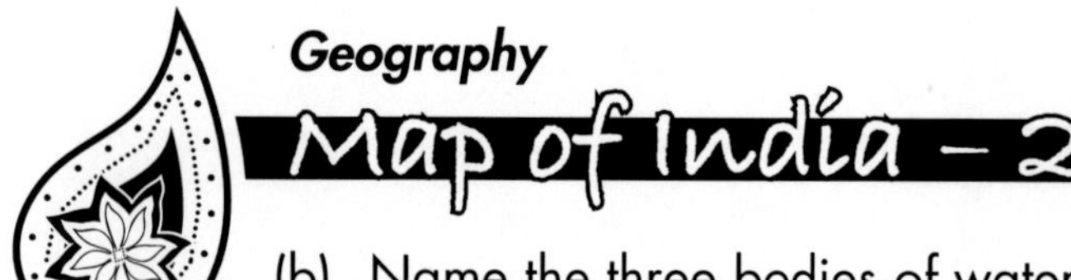

(b) Name the three bodies of water which meet the coast of India.

(c) Name the southern- and northern-most cities in India.

3. Use the map to complete this table.

State	Capital	State	Capital
Andhra Pradesh		Maharashtra	
Arunachal Pradesh		Manipur	
Assam		Meghalaya	
Bihar		Mizoram	
Chhattisgarh		Nagaland	
Goa		Orissa	
Gujarat		Punjab	*Chandigarh*
Haryana	*Chandigarh*	Rajasthan	
Himachal Pradesh		Sikkim	
Jammu and Kashmir		Tamil Nadu	
Jharkhand		Tripura	
Karnataka		Uttarakhand	
Kerala		Uttar Pradesh	
Madhya Pradesh		West Bengal	
Union territory	**Capital**	**Union territory**	**Capital**
Andaman and Nicobar Islands		National Capital Territory of Delhi	*Delhi*
Chandigarh	—	Lakshadweep	
Dadra and Nagar Haveli		Puducherry	*Puducherry*
Daman and Diu			

Map of India – 3

4. **Look at the map on page 3 and the table you completed for Question 3. What two facts do you notice about Chandigarh?**

   (a) ____

   ____

   (b) ____

   ____

5. **What type of features are being displayed on the map below?**

   ____

   ____

   ____

   ____

6. **What is the name of the ...**

   (a) desert to the north?

   ____

   (b) main river?

   ____

   (c) capital of India?

   ____

   (d) mountain range which separates north from south?

   ____

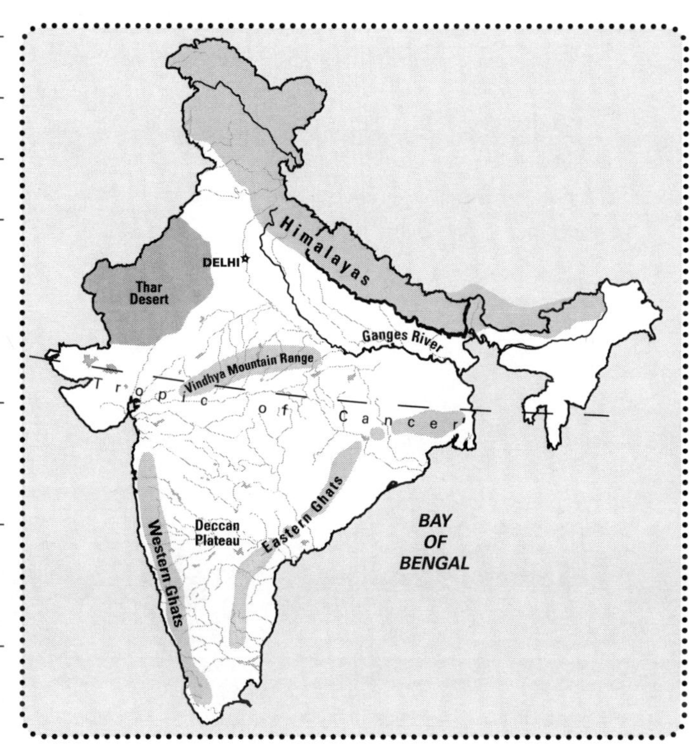

   (e) major circle of latitude which crosses India? _______________________________________

   (f) bay to the east of India? _______________________________________

7. **Select the location for each of these.**

   (a) capital of India

northern India	*southern India*

   (b) Deccan Plateau

northern India	*southern India*

   (c) Ganges River

northern India	*southern India*

   (d) Himalayas

northern India	*southern India*

   (e) Eastern Ghats

northern India	*southern India*

   (f) Thar Desert

northern India	*southern India*

Objectives

- Reads information about the climate in India and extracts information to complete tasks.
- Uses mapping skills to make a legend, locate named places and show areas where particular natural disasters occur.

Teacher information

- Even though India has extreme weather conditions, the people have managed to develop successful strategies to use the weather and climate to their advantage. Alpine regions are used for grazing, while rice terraces and orchards are found in the foothills of the region. To the east, where there is more rainfall, farmers grow rice, buckwheat and barley. Farmers in the west use the drier conditions to grow winter wheat, rice in summer, cotton, sugar cane and sorghum (a type of cereal and a source of grain for livestock). The dry areas of the desert have been developed by farmers to grow cotton, while the south-west corner of India contains coconut groves, fishing, rice fields, tapioca, millet and pulses.
- The monsoons bring floods which can break the banks of the Ganges; however, this washes important nutrient-rich silt onto farm areas which support strong farm growth.

Answers

1. Teacher check

2.

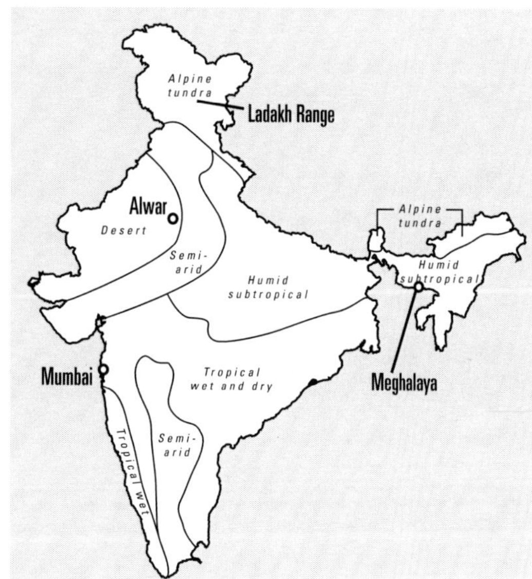

3. Teacher check

4.

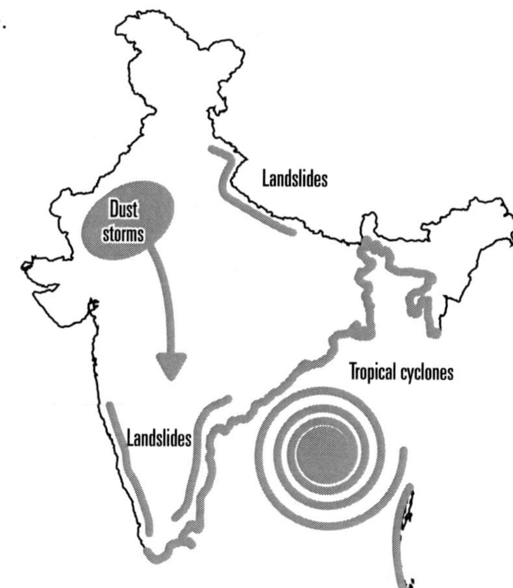

Additional activity

- Present a news report on a natural disaster which has occurred overnight in India. Use video to replicate a foreign correspondent communicating with the 'anchor' back in the studio.

Climate and natural disasters

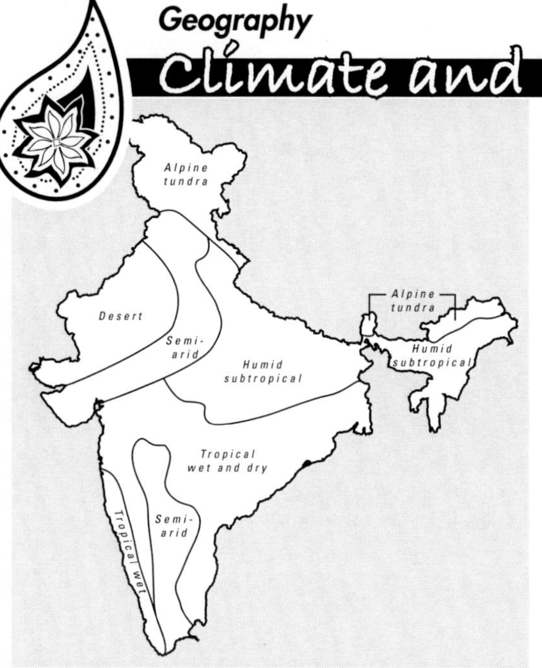

India's amazing geography creates a variety of climatic conditions across the nation. It boasts six different climatic zones across the mainland and islands.

1. Create a colour-coded legend and use it to colour the map.

Alpine tundra		Desert
Humid subtropical		Semi-arid
Tropical wet and dry		Tropical wet

The majority of people in India experience four distinct seasons—winter (January to February), summer (March to May), monsoon (June to September) and post-monsoon (October to December).

The most significant is the monsoon season—a time of heavy and consistent rainfall. The monsoon is welcomed by farmers; however, it can also have devastating effects as riverbanks break and surrounding areas flood. On the opposite end of the scale, western India has experienced some of the hottest temperatures on record; while in the north, heavy snowfalls can cause deadly landslides.

2. Locate each place mentioned in the Extreme weather facts. Plot them clearly on the map above.

3. On the table below, use a different colour to show when each season occurs.

January	February	March	April
May	June	July	August
September	October	November	December

India's intense and varied climatic conditions also lead to intense natural disasters such as floods, landslides, tropical cyclones, droughts and dust storms. Droughts are generally related to the El Niño phenomenon, which directly affects agriculture in India, as farmers rely heavily on the monsoonal rains. Heavy rain and snow has been responsible for deadly landslides in the Himalayas to the north and the Western and Eastern Ghats ranges to the south. Heavy dust storms initiate in the north-west corner and travel southward, depositing arid soil across India. The south-east corner of India (including its islands) are regularly battered by severe tropical cyclones—bringing storm surges, heavy rain and intense winds.

4. On this blank map of India, show the following:

(a) The pathway of the dust storms.

(b) Areas affected by landslides.

(c) Regions affected by tropical cyclones.

Extreme weather!

- The Ladakh Range, in the north, has experienced temperatures as low as –45 °C.
- Alwar, in Rajesthan, recorded an incredibly hot 50.6 °C in 1955.
- Mawsynram, Meghalaya, has experienced the highest annual rainfall of any place on Earth—1690 mm.
- Part of Mumbai suffered through 104.5 cm (!) of rain in just one day on 26 July 2005.

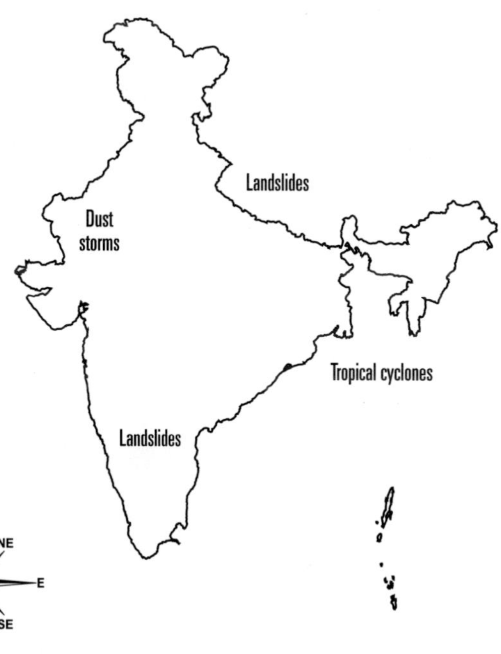

Geography

Population and language

Objectives

- Reads and understands information provided in text, table and graph form.
- Uses graphing skills to create a graph and extract information from graphs.

Teacher information

- Sanskrit is a complex language which involves inflections, changes of vowels and sound modification depending on context. This is probably why so many languages and dialects have been developed from this one language.

Answers

1.

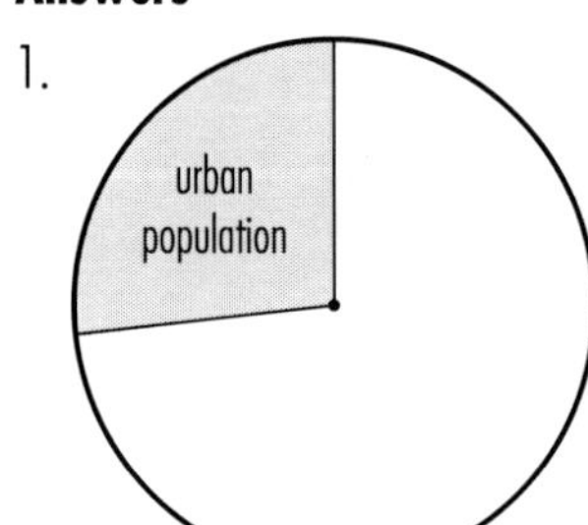

2. Total population of Mumbai and Delhi = 26 181 355; 2.24% of India's total population live in Mumbai and Delhi. (To calculate: Total population of Mumbai and Delhi divided by India's total population, multiplied by 100.)

3. Even though India is only the seventh largest country on Earth, it has the second largest population. This means that it has more people per square kilometre than most other countries.

4. (a) Hindi with 41%   (b) Malayalam and Oriya with 3.2% each
   (c) 69 030 000 people in India speak Tamil.
      (To calculate: Total population of India multiplied by the percentage (5.9%/.059) of people who speak Tamil.)

Additional activity

- Use the Internet to research India's population density by state and union territory. Create a legend and colour a blank map of India to show the distribution of India's population.

     India   Prim-Ed Publishing® — www.prim-ed.com

Population and Language

India is ranked the second-most populated country in the world, behind China, with a population of approximately 1.17 billion people. The population of India accounts for about 17.23 per cent of the world's total population.

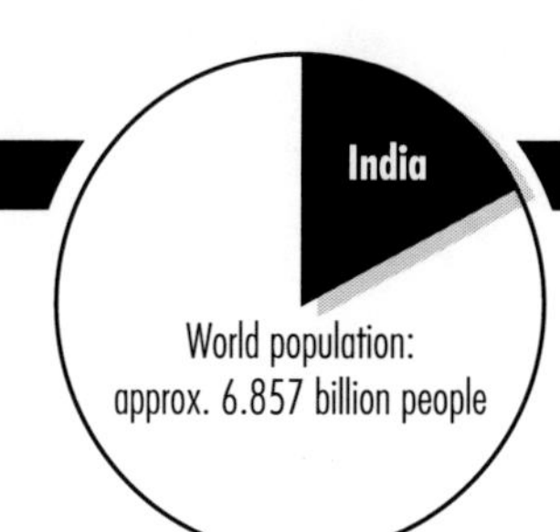

World population:
approx. 6.857 billion people

Rank	City	Country	Population
1	Shanghai	China	15 968 867
2	Mumbai	India	13 922 125
3	Karachi	Pakistan	12 827 927
4	Delhi	India	12 259 230
5	Buenos Aires	Argentina	12 197 347

In terms of size, India is the seventh largest country in the world, accounting for about 2.2 per cent of Earth's land area.

India can also boast having two of the most populated cities in the world. However, for such highly populated cities, 73 per cent of India's population actually live in the rural regions of India.

1. **Show the proportion of people who live in the urban areas of India on this pie chart.**

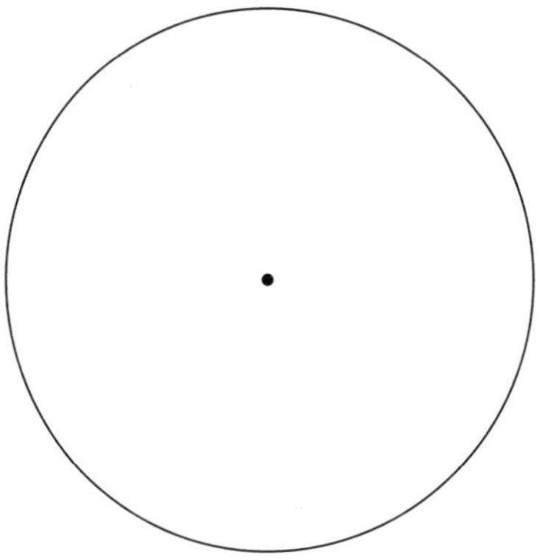

2. **Calculate the total population of India's two most populated cities. Also, calculate what percentage of India's total population live in these two cities.**

3. **Think about the total area of India and its total population in relation to the rest of the world. What comments could you make?**

____

____

Language in India is directly related to cultural beliefs and defines communities. The oldest spoken language in India is Sanskrit. It is the language which gave birth to the 1652 different languages and their dialects spoken in India today.

4. **Look at the pie graph.**

    (a) Which language is spoken most?

    ____

    (b) Which two languages are equally popular?

    ____

    (c) How many people in India speak Tamil? _________________________________

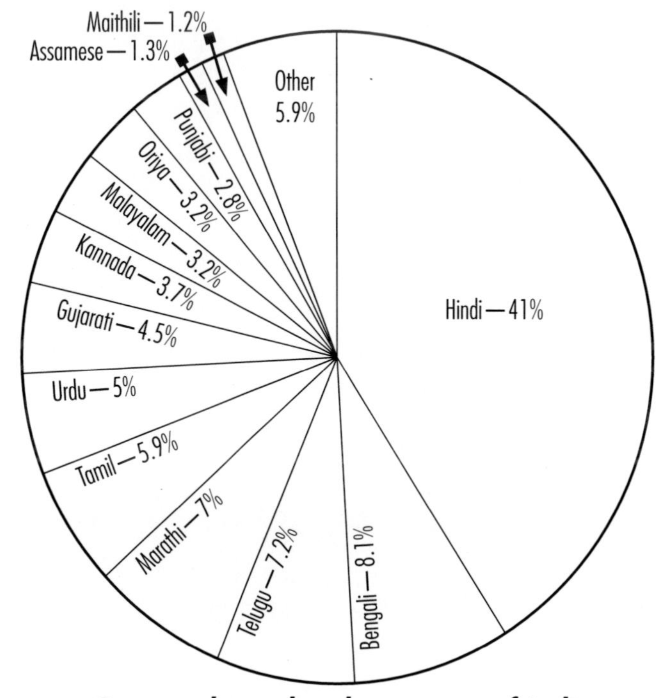

Commonly spoken languages of India

The Himalayas and the Ganges .... pages 11–13

Objectives

- Reads information about the Himalaya Mountains and the Ganges River and extracts information to complete tasks.
- Uses information from the text to make his or her own conclusions of possible future outcomes.

Teacher information

- The Ganges River may begin fresh, clean and pure in the Himalayas; however, by the time it reaches the Bay of Bengal, it is a combination of untreated sewage, decomposing bodies, rubbish, fertilisers and pesticides from farming, and industrial waste. Animals wade and bathe in the river, people bathe and wash their clothes in the river and they also use the water for drinking and cooking. It is believed that thousands of people die each year in India due to waterborne disease. Fishers who have relied on the Ganges River for their livelihood are increasingly without work as the high levels of pollution have impacted on the number of fish in the river.
- The Ganga Action Plan was brought into effect in April 1985. Its purpose was to reduce the amount of raw, untreated sewage entering the Ganges. However, not a lot of change has occurred over the years since. India has few environmental regulations, which contributes to the high level of pollution. Industry is required to pay a small fee to the government to be allowed to dump unmonitored waste into the river.

Answers

Page 13

1. See crossword
2. Teacher check
3. Answers should be similar to: If there is less water in the Ganges, then farming and people's lives will be impacted. There would be water shortages, which would make life for the millions of people who rely on the river very difficult.
4. 8850 m + (1 cm x 100 = 1m) = 8851 m

Additional activity

- The Ganges is suffering from the effects of pollution. Research to find out the negative effects of pollution on the Ganges, the wildlife which relies on the Ganges for life and the people of India. Devise a possible plan which may help the Ganges and the animals and people which rely on it for life.

Crossword answers: BAY OF BENGAL, GANGA, SIKKIM, GODS, SEDIMEN (SEDIMENT), HOLY, TRIVENI, SIX, GANGETIC PLAIN, GHATS, RANGE, HINDU, SHRINES, BATHE, VARANASI, CAVE, HIMALAYAS, YAMUNA, GANGES DELTA, GANGOTRI, PILGRIMS

The Himalayas and the Ganges – 1

The Ganges River begins life in the highest mountain range in the world—the Himalaya Mountains. It flows for 2510 kilometres, travelling south-east across northern India, and completes its epic journey in the world's largest delta at the Bay of Bengal.

The Himalaya Mountains

For 70 million years, the Indian subcontinent has been drifting northward, 'crashing' into Asia. This movement is responsible for the formation of the world's youngest mountain range—what we call the Himalayas or Himalaya Mountains.

The Himalayas stretch 2400 kilometres across six countries, including India. It is the highest mountain range in the world, with more than 100 mountains over 7200 metres tall; the tallest being Mount Everest, reaching a staggering 8850 metres above sea level.

The Indian subcontinent is still moving northward at a rate of about 67 mm each year, causing the Himalayas to grow at an approximate rate of 1 cm each year.

Kangchenjunga (8586 m) is the third tallest peak within the Himalayas and can be found on the border of India and Nepal. It comprises five peaks, three of which are located in the Indian state of Sikkim. Its name means 'the five treasures of snows'; the treasures represent gold, silver, gems, grain and holy books—one treasure for each peak.

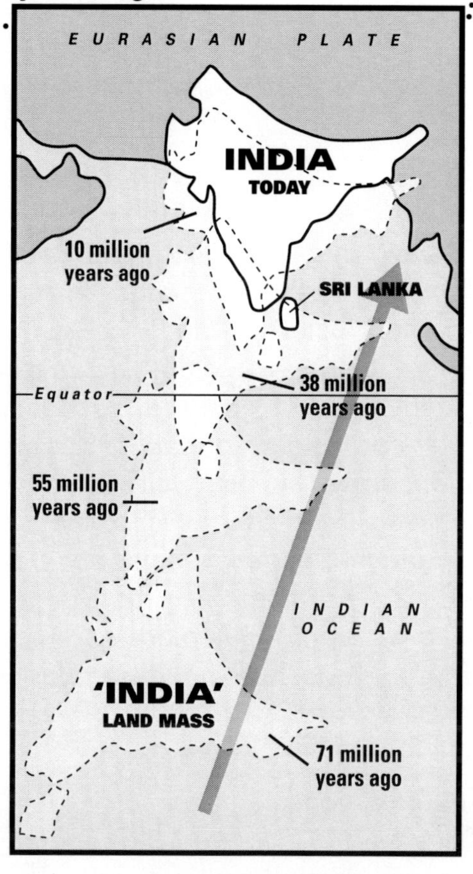

The peaks of the Himalayas are covered with snow all year round and are home to around 15 000 glaciers—the source of many rivers. The Gangotri Glacier, located in the Indian state of Uttarakhand, is believed to feed into the Ganges River.

The Ganges

Water from the Himalayas ('the land of the gods') runs down to feed into the Ganges. Much of the water in the Ganges comes from the fresh water stored as ice and snow in the Himalayas and its glaciers. The rest of the water comes from the heavy monsoons which begin in mid-June.

It is difficult to say that one single source gives rise to the Ganges, as many smaller rivers join together in its beginning stages to form this magnificent river, which supports one-tenth of the world's population.

The goddess, Ganga

The Hindu religion evolved along the banks of the Ganges (as the goddess, Ganga) and many beliefs and festivals centre around the water of the Ganges. The source of the Ganges is sacred to the Hindu religion and many sacred shrines and temples have been constructed at various holy points along its path. Hindu people believe they must bathe in its waters at least once in their lifetime; it is also considered important to collect and store some of this most holy water in their homes. The Hindu people believe the water of the Ganges to have supernatural powers and the ability to cleanse the sins of the soul and to heal the sick.

The Himalayas and the Ganges – 2

One of the most significant locations is Goumukh (an ice cave), the point at which the Gangotri Glacier gives birth to the Bhagirathi River (the primary source stream of the Ganges). This location is considered extremely holy by devout Hindus, who regularly make the pilgrimage to bathe in its freezing waters.

At Devprayag, the Bhagirathi River merges with the Alaknanda River, the second tributary of the Ganges. This is where the river becomes known as the Ganges (or Ganga). The Alaknanda River carries a great deal of sediment into the river system, which is carried south-east and contributes to the fertile soil of the Gangetic Plain. Each point where rivers merge into the Ganges is considered a holy place and many devout Hindus will make the pilgrimage.

The next significant location on the Ganges is at Allahabad, where the Yamuna River joins the Ganga. The Yamuna River begins life in the Yamunotri Glacier in the Himalayas. Hindus consider the Yamuna River to be very sacred and bathing in it is common practice for devout Hindus. The point where the two holy rivers meet is called the 'Triveni Sangam'. It is believed that drops of nectar fell there from the pitcher of the gods and that bathing there washes away all sins and clears the way to heaven.

At the city of Patna, the Ganges River is joined by four rivers: Ghagra, Gandak, Punpun and Sone. Patna is famous for the Mahatma Gandhi Setu bridge over the Ganges. It stretches 5575 m across the river and is one of the longest single-river bridges in the world.

Varanasi is thought to be the oldest existing city in India, if not the world. Steps, known as 'ghats', have been built leading down to the Ganges River so that pilgrims can easily bathe in the holy waters. Many temples have been constructed in this city—for it is considered the holiest of holy places along the Ganges. It is at this point that the Ganges changes direction, travelling north-east.

At the end of its magnificent journey, the Ganges then enters Bangladesh and forms the Ganges Delta. The delta is the largest on Earth, covering 105 000 km. At this point the fresh river water mixes with sea water and mangroves are subjected to the tides of the ocean. The Ganges has travelled from the snowy peaks of the Himalayas to the tropical mangroves of the Bay of Bengal.

The Himalayas and the Ganges—3

1. Use the information provided in the texts to complete this puzzle.

Across

3. The sea water from here welcomes the fresh water of the Ganges.
4. The other name given to the Ganges.
5. The Indian state in which you would find three of the 'five treasures'.
9. A large geographical area of India with the most fertile of soil.
10. The Himalayas is the highest mountain _______ in the world.
11. A person who follows Hinduism.
14. Goumukh is where pilgrims _______ in the freezing water.
15. The Himalayas stretch across this number of countries.
16. The youngest mountain range in the world.
17. This river begins life in the Yamunotri Glacier.
18. The largest of its kind on Earth, covering an area of 105 000 km.
19. The special name given to those who travel to a particular place for religious purposes.

Down

1. Home to one of the world's longest single-river bridges.
2. The Alaknanda River contributes this to the Ganges and the Gangetic Plain.
4. The Himalayas is known as 'the land of the _______'.
6. The water of the Ganges is considered to be very _______ by Hindu people.
7. The point where it is believed that nectar fell from the pitcher of the gods.
8. The feature you would find at Goumukh.
9. The feature constructed to make bathing in the Ganges easier for pilgrims.
12. These holy places have been constructed at significant points along the Ganges.
13. Thought to be the oldest existing city in India.

2. Reread the section titled 'The Himalaya Mountains'. Use a highlighter pen to show the most significant keywords and phrases.

3. Some scientific studies show that many of the glaciers in the Himalayas are **retreating.** *What might this mean for the Ganges and the people of India?*

____

____

____

4. Calculate the possible height of Mount Everest 100 years from now.

____

____

New Delhi .... page 15

Objectives

- Uses mapping skills to locate and highlight particular places on a map.
- Reads and understands text about New Delhi in order to answer quiz questions.

Teacher information

- Colonial rule of Indian was transferred to the British Crown in 1858, under Queen Victoria. During this time, India was known as the Indian Empire and, after 1877, Queen Victoria was proclaimed the Empress of India.
- British rule ceased in 1947 and India became an independent republic. Being a republic, India's head of state is a president, who is elected for a five-year term.

Answers

1. Teacher check

2. (a) Calcutta   (b) architect   (c) 1400BCE

Additional activities

- Research to find out more about the parliament of India. Draw up a comparison chart, comparing Indian parliament to the government of your country.
- Create a tourist map of New Delhi, highlighting special sightseeing places of interest.

New Delhi

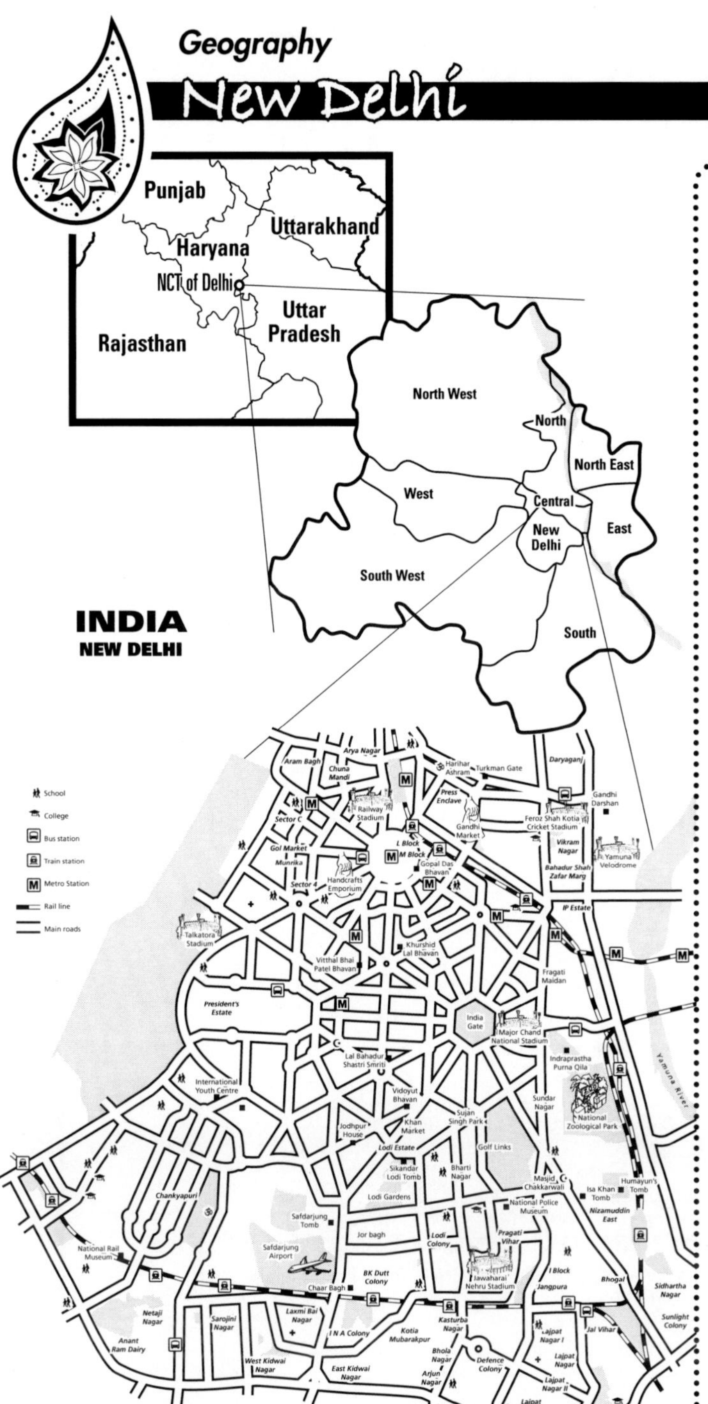

New Delhi is a small area within the National Capital Territory of Delhi, which is located in northern India to the west of the Yamuna River (which later joins the Ganges).

New Delhi was built to the south of Old Delhi and covers an area of 42.7 km². It houses the Indian parliament, public offices, museums and monuments. The city was planned in 1912 by Edwin Lutyens and Herbert Baker, both British architects, and took a construction contractor, Sobha Singh, his son and a construction team about 13 years to construct.

New Delhi may be a recent addition to Delhi, however, ancient artefacts suggest humans lived in the region thousands of years ago. Records show that Indraprastha (the original city) was built by a Pandava king about 1400 BCE. Since then, many rulers and dynasties have fought to rule the capital of India.

New Delhi has been the capital of India since December 1911, when the British decided it would be easier to govern India from Delhi rather than Calcutta (Kolkata), the capital of India at that time.

Delhi, within which New Delhi lies, is the second largest city in India and visitors there may hear people speaking Hindi, English, Urdu and Punjabi.

1. **Look at the three maps.**
   On the first map, locate the National Capital Territory of Delhi.
   On the second map, shade the area known as New Delhi.

2. **Answer these quick questions.**

   (a) Which Indian city was the capital of India in November 1911?

New Delhi	Indraprastha	Calcutta

   (b) Which word from the text means 'one who designs buildings'?

ruler	construction contractor	architect

   (c) People have lived in the area known as New Delhi since ...

the times of early humans.	1911.	1400 BCE.

History

Objective

Reads and comprehends information about early civilisations in India.

Teacher information

- The greatest Gupta emperor was Chandragupta II. He was known as 'Vikramaditya', meaning he had the 'power of the sun'.
- From the 12th century onwards, Muslim armies had conquered much of northern India. During this time many new inventions, foods and ideas were introduced to the India subcontinent from the Muslim peoples.
- The Mughal Empire was one of the most successful in India. Its extent was greater than that of India today.
- Read the text with the class. Clarify any difficult terms and misconceptions. It may be helpful to draw a time line on the board showing when each empire existed in India. Pupils may require further explanations of the terms BCE and CE.

Answers

1. (a) lasted for about two hundred years – Gupta Empire
   (b) the last Indian empire – Mughal Empire
   (c) Buddhism was promoted during this time – Mauryan Empire
   (d) its ancient cities are being excavated – Indus Valley civilisation

2. Answers may vary: When a king conquered many other kingdoms, he created an empire.

3. (a) 3300   (b) 700s   (c) 40   (d) 1857   (e) 700s

4. Answers may vary.
   (a) What are the names of the two main cities of the Indus Valley Civilisation?
   (b) What do scientists suggest was the reason for the decline of the Indus civilisation?
   (c) What relation was Emperor Ashoka to Chandragupta Maurya?
   (d) What was the name given to the time during the Gupta Empire where great achievements in the arts occurred?
   (e) What did the people of the Mughal Empire name India and its language?

Additional activity

- At its height, the Indus Valley Civilisation extended over 1.25 million square kilometres. On a map of Asia (or the world) mark these four points and join them in a circle to show the extent of the Indus civilisation: - Mumbai (south), Delhi (east), the Iranian border (west), the Himalayas (north).

Objectives

- Reads information about pots from the Indus Valley Civilisation.
- Uses archeological terms to describe the rim, body and base of the pots.

Teacher information

- Different methods were used to make the pots of the Indus Civilisation. Some were made by hand and others on a potter's wheel.
- Most pots, jars and plates discovered are broken into shards meaning archeologists spend much time examining the pieces to determine which type of pot they originated from. Handles on a pot reveal what it was used for and which society made it.

Answers

1. (a) inverted, globular, flat   (b) straight, carinated, flat
   (c) everted, straight-sided, flat   (d) everted, globular, flat

2.–3. Teacher check

Additional activity

- Draw the pots on coloured card and decorate them. Turn the pots into jigsaws by cutting the drawings. Ask a partner to put the pots back together.

Early civilisations in India – 1

In ancient times, India was not one country ruled by a single power. Instead there were many small kingdoms that often fought against each other to gain more land and power. When a king conquered many other kingdoms, he created an empire.

The Indus Valley Civilisation

In the north-west region of India and in the land that is now Pakistan, an ancient civilisation developed and thrived in the fertile valley of the Indus River. This civilisation—one of the earliest in the world, dating back over 5000 years ago—is credited with many discoveries and inventions in mathematics, science, industry, medicine and agriculture.

The two main cities in the civilisation were Harappa and Mohenjo-Daro. These large towns were carefully designed with paved streets in a grid-like pattern, and had systems in place for water supply and drainage.

The excavation of these archaeological sites has provided evidence of a very advanced civilisation, which had developed ways of counting and measuring, and had a written language.

A Harappan seal

In Harappa, words were represented by symbols, with each imprinted on a seal.

The Indus Valley Civilisation existed from about 3300 BCE and began to decline around 1700 BCE. Scientists today suggest that ecological disasters, such as earthquakes or flooding, may have been the reason for its decline.

The Mauryan Empire

One of India's greatest early empires was the Mauryan Empire, which covered a large part of South Asia. Emperor Ashoka (grandson of Chandragupta Maurya), who reigned from 272–232 BCE, followed and promoted Buddhism. He ordered that words of love and peace were to be carved in stone on rocks and pillars throughout the empire, so people could read the words and spread the message.

The Gupta Empire

The Gupta Empire, which lasted from approximately 319 CE to 500 CE, was part of the 'golden period' of Indian history. Great works of literature, art, drama, music, mathematics, astronomy and medicine were produced at this time.

When the Hun people invaded, the Gupta Empire collapsed and power passed from a central government to local lords and a collection of small kingdoms. Also, from the early 700s, sections of north-west India and what is now Pakistan were invaded by people from the west. These people were Islamic and brought with them the Muslim religion.

The Mughal Empire

In 1526, a prince named Babur established what was to become known as the Mughal Empire. The Mughal Empire developed from the Muslim invaders from the west. They renamed India as 'Hind' and the language 'Hindi', which, in its spoken and written form, came from the ancient language called 'Sanskrit'.

Under Emperor Akbar, who reigned from 1556–1605, almost the whole of India was part of the Mughal Empire. During this time, the country was unified as one nation and prospered.

The empire began to decline at the beginning of the 18th century, but it was the British who displaced the last Mughal emperor, Bahadur Shah II, in 1857.

Early civilisations in India – 2

1. Match the fact to the civilisation or empire it refers to.

   (a) lasted for about two hundred years   •   • Mughal Empire

   (b) the last Indian empire   •   • Indus Valley Civilisation

   (c) Buddhism was promoted during this time •   • Gupta Empire

   (d) its ancient cities are being excavated   •   • Mauryan Empire

2. Briefly explain how an empire was 'created'.

____

____

____

3. Write numbers to complete these sentences.

(a) The Indus Valley Civilisation began around _____________ BCE.

(b) The first Muslims arrived in India in the early _____________.

(c) The reign of Emperor Ashoka lasted for _____________ years.

(d) In _____________, Britain deposed of the last Mughal Emperor.

(e) The Gupta Empire began its decline in the early _____________.

4. Use information from the text to write a question for these answers.

(a) Ans: Harappa and Mohenjo-Daro

   Qu: _______________________________________

____

(b) Ans: ecological disasters

   Qu: _______________________________________

____

(c) Ans: his grandson

   Qu: _______________________________________

____

(d) Ans: the 'golden period'

   Qu: _______________________________________

____

(e) Ans: Hind and Hindi

   Qu: _______________________________________

____

Bahadur Shah II:
The last Mughal emperor

The pots of the Indus Valley

Many interesting objects have been discovered at the archeological sites of the Indus Valley Civilisation, the most common being different types of pots. The type of clay used, the decoration on the pots and how each was manufactured gives archeologists and historians much information about life in the Indus Valley.

*The three main parts of a pot are the **rim**, the **body** and the **base**.*

* *The rim is at the opening at the top of the pot. There are three main types of rim: **straight**, **inverted** (turning inward) and **everted** (turning outward).*

* *The design of the body shows what the pot was used for (holding either liquids or solids). Bodies can be described as **globular** (spherical), **carinated** (keel-shaped) or **straight-sided**.*

* *The base (the bottom of the pot) can be either flat or rounded.*

1. Study these Indus Valley pots and circle the best words to describe them.

(a) Pot 1

Rim	Body	Base
straight	globular	flat
inverted	carinated	rounded
everted	straight-sided	

(b) Pot 2

Rim	Body	Base
straight	globular	flat
inverted	carinated	rounded
everted	straight-sided	

(c) Pot 3

Rim	Body	Base
straight	globular	flat
inverted	carinated	rounded
everted	straight-sided	

(d) Pot 4

Rim	Body	Base
straight	globular	flat
inverted	carinated	rounded
everted	straight-sided	

2. Choose one pot and describe what you think it was used for.

Pot ______ : ____

____

3. Use clay or plasticine™ to sculpt the four types of Indus Valley pots.

History

Objective

- Reads and completes information about British rule, India gaining independence and the partition of India.

Teacher information

- Despite their dislike of the British, India fought with them in both world wars.
- The British rule in India came in two parts:
  - 1757–1858: when the British East India Company virtually abandoned its trading enterprise and established Company Rule after the Battle of Plassey.
  - 1858–1947: when the company was dissolved and its rule transferred to the British Crown.
- In 1937, the province of Burma — to the east of the Indian Empire — became a separate colony, gaining independence in 1948.
- In 1947, the British Indian Empire was partitioned into two sovereign dominion states:
  - the Union of India, which later became the Republic of India.
  - the Dominion of Pakistan, which later became the Islamic Republic of Pakistan.
- In 1971, East Pakistan became the People's Republic of Bangladesh.

Answers

1. (a) True (b) True (c) False (d) False
2. (a) attacks (b) laws (c) Britain (d) Pakistan
3. Answers may vary:

   dissolved — to bring to an end; terminate

   discrimination — unfair treatment of a person, racial group or minority

   unrest — a rebellious state of discontent

   exploit — to take advantage of a person or situation for one's own ends

   independence — freedom from control or influence of others

   boycotting — (boycott) to refuse to deal with an organisation or country as a protest against its actions or policies

   advocated — (advocate) to recommend a course of action publicly

   nonviolent — (nonviolence) abstaining from the use of violence

   resistance — the act of resisting (to strive to offset the actions, effects, or force of)

   partition — (in the case of India) to divide into separate self-governing parts

   migrate — to move from one country or region and settle in another

   refugee — a person who has fled from danger, such as war or political persecution

Additional activity

- Imagine you and your family were ordered to leave your home and migrate to a new country. If you could only carry a small backpack with you on your journey, what would you fill it with? Write a list.

Turbulent times in India's history

The British first arrived in India when the British East India Company set up a trading post there. For almost 2500 years, the kingdoms of India fought many battles against the company as it made its way across the country, taking control of their land and people.

When, in 1858, Queen Victoria **dissolved** the British East India Company, she was given the name Empress of India. But in the years that followed, the British government failed to follow the Queen's wishes and the Indian people continued to suffer great **discrimination**. The unfair treatment caused much **unrest** in the country and the British feared attacks. To weaken their opposition, the British decided to **exploit** the already-existing tension between two groups in India—the Muslims and the Hindus—setting them against each other.

But Britain had ruled India for too long and it was time for its people to be free! The Indian people began the long road to **independence** by **boycotting** British goods and disobeying the British laws they considered to be discriminatory.

Mahatma Gandhi, a peaceful, spiritual leader, **advocated nonviolent** methods of **resistance**, and played a major role in the negotiations which led to India winning its independence from Britain on 15 August, 1947.

However, after independence, the violent conflict between Hindus and Muslims escalated. This resulted in the **partition** of the country. Sections of India separated from it to form a new nation, the Muslim country of, Pakistan. The millions of Hindus living there were forced to flee to India, and millions of Muslims living in India were made to **migrate** to Pakistan. During this enormous population exchange, it is estimated that half a million people died from violence, starvation, the difficult journey and the hardship of being a **refugee**.

1. **Choose if each sentence is true or false.**

   (a) Indians resisted the advances of the *British East India Company*.   **True**   **False**

   (b) Queen Victoria wanted fair treatment of India's people.   **True**   **False**

   (c) Under British rule, India was a united, peaceful country.   **True**   **False**

   (d) To gain independence, Indians began violent attacks.   **True**   **False**

2. **Complete the sentences.**

   (a) The British Government caused unrest as they feared _______________________.

   (b) To show their contempt, Indians ignored unfair British _______________________.

   (c) On 15 August 1947, India won its independence from _______________________.

   (d) Millions of Muslims were forced to leave India and move to _______________________.

3. **Choose six of the twelve words in bold text above. On the back of this sheet, write a definition for each.**

History

Objective

Reads and comprehends information about Indian inventions and discoveries.

Teacher information

- Other discoveries and inventions attributed to (or refined by) India include the autocannon and multi-barrel gun, bounce lighting (devised and used by cinematographer Subrata Mitra from 1955–1959), devices for carding for the textile industry, a version of the cotton gin (a machine for separating the fibres of cotton from the seeds), the crescograph (a device for measuring the growth of plants), types of crucible/wootz steel, the dyke, the maritime dock, the furnace, hospitals, iron, muslin, the use of microorganisms to treat oil spills, optical fibre, the pagoda, the oven, the animal-drawn plough, prefabricated homes and moveable structures, puppets and puppetry, reservoirs, iron-cased and metal-cylinder rocket artillery, the seamless celestial globe, sewage collection and disposal systems, the foot stirrup and urban planning.

- The contribution of Indian scientists and mathematicians to their fields cannot be underestimated. Other notable discoveries which are possibly of Indian origin include the decimal number system, zero, the word 'algorithm', negative numbers, Pi, precise celestial calculations, astronomical time spans, the magnetic interface balance and many others. An Indian language, Sanskrit, is the most suitable for computer language.

Answers

1. (a) chess, ludo, badminton, dice   (b) cashmere, calico   (c) dentistry, hospitals, plastic surgery

2. pyjamas, badminton

3. (a) False   (b) True   (c) True   (d) False   (e) False

4. (a) clothing such as: jumpers, cardigans, scarfs, pashmina shawls (made from the wool of the pashmina goat in Kashmir, India)
   (b) shopping bags, clothing, craft etc.

5. As the street of the two main cities in the Indus Valley, Harappa and Mohenjo-daro, were carefully planned in a grid-like pattern and had sophisticated systems for water supply and drainage in place, it is possible that these towns were the world's first examples of urban planning.

6. (a) – (b) Answers will vary

Additional activities

- Plan, design and make a new type of dice. Test your dice by using it to play a board game.
- Write a report detailing the process of gathering and manufacturing cashmere.

Objective

Designs a poster advertising a fictional museum of artefacts invented in India.

Teacher information

- Pupils can use the Internet or resource centre to find photographs of Ancient Indian artefacts, or they can draw what they imagine the artefacts (such as an Ancient Indian dentist's drilling tool) look like.

- Hold a discussion with the class about museums and ask pupils who have visited museums to share their experiences and knowledge with the class. For example: tours and tour guides, presentations etc.

Answers

Teacher check

Additional activity

- Create a cartoon strip (with speech and thought bubbles) showing the incredible discovery of the Indus Valley Civilisation in India.

Indian inventions – 1

Indian history dates back to more than 5000 years ago. The earliest large-scale settlement in India started in the rich soils of the valley of the Indus River. Excavations of archeological sites in the Indus Valley have provided evidence of a very advanced civilisation which used many of the following inventions as part of everyday life.

The ancient city of Harappa

The two largest cities in the Indus Valley, Harappa and Mohenjo-daro, were carefully designed with paved streets set in a grid-like pattern. Systems were in place for water supply and drainage, providing evidence that these cities may be the world's earliest examples of **urban planning**.

Evidence of the use of drills (probably used by skilled craftsmen) to fix tooth-related problems indicate that **dentistry** and its tools may also have begun in India.

When noses were amputated as a form of punishment, skin and tissue from other parts of the body were used to replace it. Is this the first example of **plastic surgery**?

The people of Harappa created new techniques in **metallurgy**, using the metals copper, bronze, lead and tin.

Also excavated from the Indus Valley were **bangles** made from shell, copper, bronze, gold, silver, stone and ceramics. Also, seashells were used as buttons.

During the Mauryan Empire, between 273 and 232 BCE, Emperor Ashoka established a chain of buildings throughout his empire to help sick people and animals—possibly the world's first **hospitals**.

Materials including **calico** (a type of cotton material) and **cashmere** wool (a fine wool from the cashmere goat from the area of Kashmir in the north-western region) are also of Indian origin.

In more recent history, **pyjamas** were adapted from the loose comfortable outdoor clothing worn by Indians. The British who inhabited India decided to create similar garments to sleep in.

Various toys and games existed in ancient India, including an oblong **dice** with one to six holes on its faces.

As the words for **chess** are from the Indian language Sanskrit, it is believed the game started in India and spread to other countries, through traders when India was invaded.

Snakes and ladders began as a game teaching morality (rules for good conduct), and evidence of the game of **ludo** (pachisi) was discovered on cave drawings believed to be from the 6th century CE.

Derived from a game named poona, **badminton** was played in India during the 1860s. The British army learned the game and took the equipment back to England, where the sport, known as 'the Badminton game', became popular among the British upper class.

As archeologists continue to dig and historians keep investigating, who knows how many other modern appliances, tools and objects may have begun as a part of everyday life in ancient India?

Indian inventions – 2

1. List the inventions which fit in the following categories.

(a) games: ____

(b) type of material: _______________________________________

(c) medicine: ____

2. Which two Indian inventions were greatly liked by the British?

- _________________________________   - _________________________________

3. Choose if each question is true or false.

(a) Pachisi is another name for the game of badminton.	*True*	*False*
(b) A range of metals were produced and used in Ancient India.	*True*	*False*
(c) Emperor Ashoka was dedicated to healing the sick.	*True*	*False*
(d) The original 'snake and ladders' promoted unruly behaviour.	*True*	*False*
(e) There are no more ancient Indian artefacts to be discovered.	*True*	*False*

4. Name one use of these materials in modern society.

(a) cashmere: _____________________   (b) calico: _____________________

5. What evidence is there that urban planning existed in ancient India?

____

____

____

6. (a) Rate these inventions from 1 (most significant) to 15 (least significant).

Invention	Rating	Invention	Rating	Invention	Rating
badminton		chess		metallurgy	
bangles		dentistry		plastic surgery	
buttons		dice		pyjamas	
cashmere		hospitals		snake & ladders	
calico		ludo		urban planning	

(b) Give reasons for your choices below.

- My 'number 1' choice is

  ____

  because _______________________

  ____

  _________________________________ .

- My 'number 15' choice is

  ____

  because _______________________

  ____

  _________________________________ .

The museum of Indian inventions

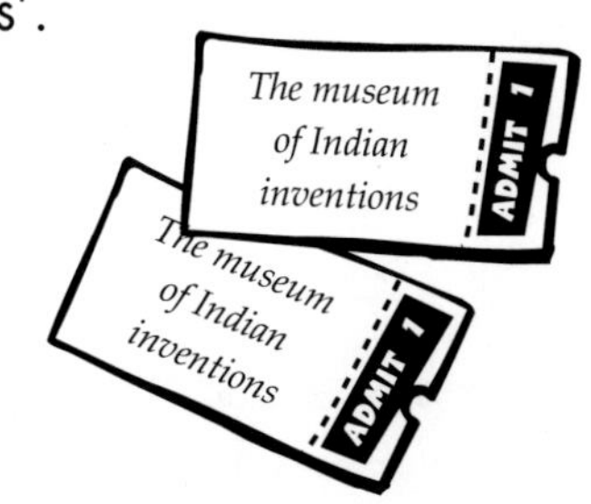

Create a poster advertising 'The museum of Indian inventions'.

Your poster must include:

- the name of the museum
- sketches of some of the artefacts displayed
- interesting facts about the artefacts and of life in ancient India
- times and names of tours and/or presentations at the museum

Your poster must be eye-catching so as to encourage people to visit the museum.

History

Objectives

- Reads information about the traditional Indian street game, gilli-danda.
- Lists the similarities and differences between gilli-danda and the game of cricket.

Teacher information

- Most traditional Indian games are inexpensive and simple, making them popular in the poorer rural areas. In cities, many of the traditional games are dying out as modern sports take their place.
- Gilli-danda, known by many other names across India and the world, has many different variations of play.
- International tournaments of gilli-danda are played between India and Pakistan.
- The danda is often handmade by the player.

Answers

2. Teacher check.
3. Answers will vary.

Additional activities

- In small groups, create a list of sports which are similar to cricket. Is there another sport which is also similar to gilli-danda? Write a list of similar sports. (Note: Gilli-danda is often called 'Indian baseball'.)
- Find out about three more traditional Indian games.
    - kabaddi
    - kho-kho
    - pithoo
- Choose the one which could be easily learnt and played by your class. Practise playing it.

Gilli-danda versus cricket

1. Read the description of this popular traditional Indian street game.

Gilli-danda

*Gilli-danda is played in an open area using two wooden sticks—a **gilli** (about 7 cm long with tapered ends) and a **danda** (about 60 cm long).*

A circle is drawn on the ground and a small oval-shaped hole (called the pillow) is dug in the centre. The gilli is placed across or inside the pillow.

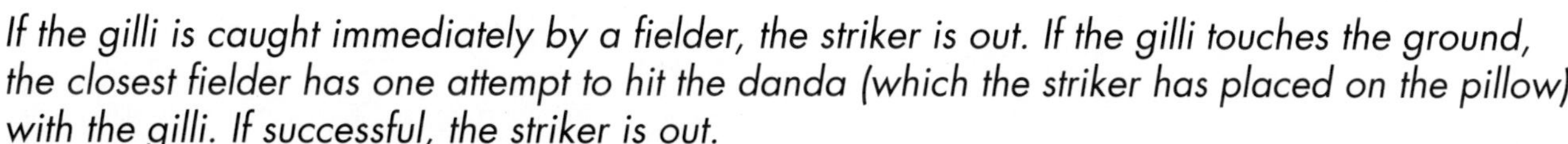

Two teams are chosen—the 'strikers' and the 'fielders'. A striker taps the gilli at one end so it becomes airborne, allowing him or her to try to strike it with great force. The aim is to hit the gilli as far as possible and away from the fielders. Strikers have three attempts to hit the gilli before being given 'out'.

If the gilli is caught immediately by a fielder, the striker is out. If the gilli touches the ground, the closest fielder has one attempt to hit the danda (which the striker has placed on the pillow) with the gilli. If successful, the striker is out.

The distance from the pillow to where the gilli lands is measured in 'danda lengths', where each length equals one point. The game continues until all players have taken a turn at striking. Any number of players can be involved in the game and the team with the higher score wins.

Many people believe cricket originated from the Indian game of gilli-danda.

2. With a partner, discuss how the game of cricket is played. Make a list of similarities and differences between Gilli-danda and cricket.

Similarities	Differences

3. (a) Do you think cricket originated from gilli-danda?   **Yes   No**

   (b) On the back of this sheet, explain your answer.

Symbols

The flag and the Sarnath Lion..page 29

Objective

Reads and uses information to produce labelled diagrams.

Teacher information

- The quote from Mahatma Gandhi has been included to remind pupils of the diverse cultures and religions in India and the unifying effect of having one national flag. Given this diversity, the symbolism of the different features of the flag assumes greater relevance. It also explains to some extend the significance and importance of the flag for so many of India's people. Because they fought hard for independence and unity, their flag is a enduring symbol of (as their first prime minister described at the time) 'freedom for all'.

- Originally, the green of the flag was linked to the Muslim religion, the saffron to the Hindu and the chakra Wheel of Law to Buddhists. The flag's colours are now seen more as symbols of courage, sacrifice, renunciation, peace, purity, truth, faith and fertility.

- India's national emblem, based on the Lion Capital of Ashoka has a motto written below it. The motto is *Satyameva Jayate,* which means 'Truth alone triumphs'. The Ashoka Chakra, the ancient Buddhist 'Wheel of Law', has 24 spokes but some other dharma chakras (wheels) are seen with a different number of spokes.

- Pupils' comprehension of the Sarnath Lion text will depend on their understanding of the specific meaning of the terminology as used in the text. They should be encouraged to try to determine the unfamiliar meaning of words from the context of how they are used in the text, rather than by referring to a dictionary. The illustrations should be of some assistance in this task. They will be required to understand the meaning of these words in order to complete Question 2. Challenging words include: cylindrical, abacus, capital, chakra, inverted, lotus and pillar.

Additional activities

- Write an explanation of an interesting county, country, town, school, business organisation or sporting club's emblem. Describe the emblem, where it came from, what it means, why it was chosen and why you find it interesting.

- Copy a large map of the world and display it on a board. Place coloured pins in a number of different countries. Pupils working in small groups choose a country. They then use a small rectangle of paper or light card to make that country's flag and attach it near the edge of the map. Cotton thread can be used to join each country to its flag.

The flag and the Sarnath Lion

India's flag

'It will be necessary for us Indians—Hindus, Muslims, Christians, Jews, Parsis and all others for whom India is their home—to recognise a common flag to live and die for.' (Gandhi)

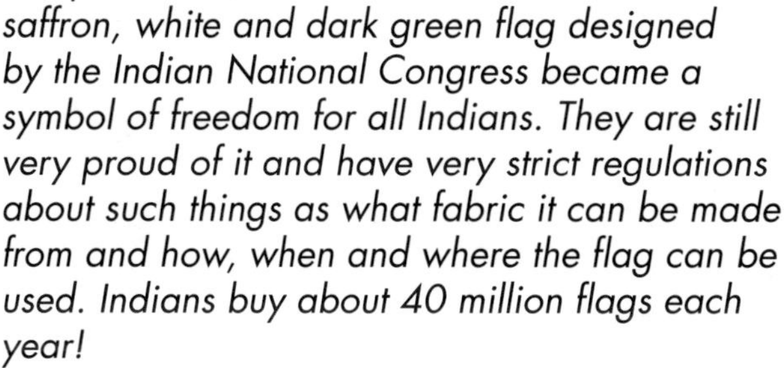

On 22 July 1947, 24 days before independence, the saffron, white and dark green flag designed by the Indian National Congress became a symbol of freedom for all Indians. They are still very proud of it and have very strict regulations about such things as what fabric it can be made from and how, when and where the flag can be used. Indians buy about 40 million flags each year!

Indian flags must be made from khadi—a hand-spun fabric of silk, cotton or wool, made popular by Gandhi. An Indian flag must never touch water or the ground or be used to cover tables or be draped over railings.

The top third of the flag is saffron, a sacred Hindu colour. It symbolises courage and sacrifice.

The white in the middle lights the path of truth and symbolises peace, purity and truth.

The green of the bottom third symbolises faith and fertility.

The Wheel of Law, the Ashoka Chakra, located in the white section of the flag, is a Buddhist symbol from 200 BCE. It is blue (for the sky and the sea) and has 24 spokes, each with a dark half moon at its end. The 24 spokes represent the 24 hours in a day and symbolise that life is in movement and death is in stagnation.

Indians are particularly proud that their flag was hoisted at the summit of Mount Everest when it was first conquered on 29 May 1953 and that on 14 November 2008, India became only the fourth country to have its flag land on the moon.

The Sarnath Lion

To celebrate 26 January 1950, the day India became a republic, a national emblem was adopted by the government.

The emblem chosen is based on the Sarnath Lion Capital of Ashoka. This capital, which is carved from a single block of black sandstone, sat on top of the Ashoka Pillar at Sarnath. It consists of four lions sitting back to back on a cylindrical abacus. The abacus had a bull, an elephant, a galloping horse and a lion carved around the outside of it. There is an Ashoka Chakra (the symbol that is on the Indian flag) carved between each animal on the abacus. Below the abacus is a very large inverted lotus flower.

King Ashoka, who ruled northern India in the third century BCE, had the pillar erected at Sarnath, the site of Buddah's first teachings. The pillar remains there in its original position, but in order to preserve the Lion Capital, it has been moved to the Sarnath Museum.

On the national emblem you can only see three of the lions and the part of the abacus with the bull and the horse on it. There is one Ashoka Chakra in the middle and a part of two others just visible on the sides. The lotus is not part of the national emblem. The motto means 'Truth alone triumphs'.

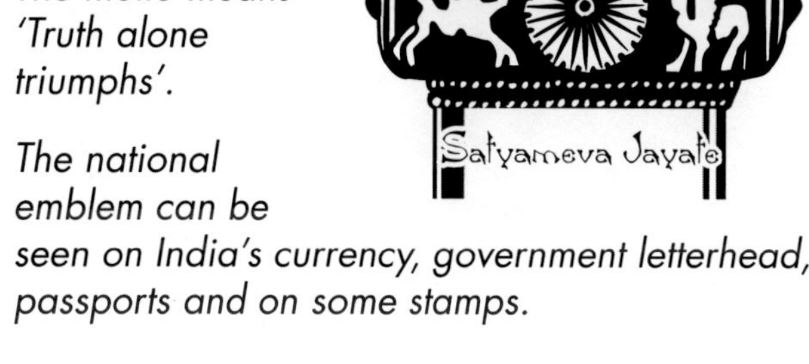

The national emblem can be seen on India's currency, government letterhead, passports and on some stamps.

---

1. **Draw and colour the Indian flag. Write relevant information about the symbolism of each part of the flag on separate squares of paper. Use lines to connect the information to the flag's parts.**

2. **Use the information in the text to draw and label a Sarnath Lion Capital on an Ashoka Pillar.**

Symbols

Objective

Reads information and plans and writes an information report.

Teacher information

- The Indian peafowl, *Pavo cristatus*, has been introduced to many parts of the world and like so many introduced species, in some places it has become feral. It is widely distributed in India, where it was once domesticated and used for food. It is now protected by the Indian Wildlife Protection Act of 1972.

- Peafowl nest and feed on the ground but fly to the tops of trees at night. They are still hunted for their feathers and sometimes poisoned, despite the parliamentary statute of protection and their status as a sacred bird. They have sometimes been described as 'urban dogs' because when kept as pets, they make a loud noise to indicate that people are approaching. Some of the stately homes in Britain keep peafowl.

- Peacocks are seen in pictures with gods and goddesses and have an ancient connection with the Hindu religion. Indra, their god of thunder, rains and war, is often portrayed as riding a peacock, and some believe there will be rain when they see one dance with its train spread. (Peafowl often mate at the beginning of the monsoon season.) The peacock is also featured in some Islamic buildings and has been used in Christianity to symbolise the resurrection.

- Pupils should use dot points when completing their report plan. They may have more information to add to their plan or refer to other sources. Their report, when written, should include the subheadings provided and any other relevant subheadings.

Additional activities

- Write and illustrate an article suitable for an Indian newspaper about a bird that is of some national significance in your country.

- Make an origami peacock (instructions are available on the internet) or describe how peacock feathers can be used in an art or craft activity.

National fauna: the Indian peacock

When it was decided in 1963 that India was to have a national bird, many Indians believed the Indian peacock was the obvious choice. This sacred bird had featured in many of their country's legends and in some of its religions, too. The peacock had been part of India's culture for centuries and was seen in many Indian arts and crafts. The people valued peacocks and believed they represented admirable qualities, such as beauty, pride, grace and mysticism.

The peafowl is one of the world's largest flying birds. About the size of a swan, the male has a distinctive fan-shaped crest and a decorative train that is more than half the bird's length. The train, which is not its tail, is made up of about 200 feathers, each with a beautifully coloured 'eye' at its end. The male fans out its brightly-coloured tail during its mating dance. A glistering blue colour is seen on the bird's long slender neck and on its breast. The peahen is smaller and is a dull greenish-grey colour and does not have a train.

Peafowl like to live in open forests near water but can be found in jungles, too. They eat grains, berries, crops, figs, insects and small reptiles and usually hunt for food at sunrise and sunset. Peahens can lay from 3 to 12 light brown eggs, but 4 to 6 is more common. They are laid two days apart and the peachicks take 28 days to hatch. Although beautiful to look at, peacocks have a harsh, unpleasant call.

At the end of every summer, a peacock loses its train feathers which many people collect and sell. Peacock feathers are valuable and although the birds have been protected since 1973, they are still killed for them. Peacocks are not hard to hunt because they usually return to the same tree every night to sleep.

1. **Use the information provided above, plus any additional information, to write brief notes in the report plan.**

Title:	Classification:
Description:	
Appearance: _________________________	
Behaviour: _________________________	
Habitat: _________________________	
Breeding: _________________________	
Conclusion:	

2. **Use your plan to write a report on a separate sheet of paper, using the headings and subheadings given. Add an appropriate illustration(s).**

National flora ....page 33

Objective

Reads and comprehends information about the national floral symbols of India.

Teacher information

- The lotus is sometimes mistaken as a water lily, but the two plants are from different families. Although the lotus grows out of mud, its flowers are extremely beautiful. This is why it is considered a symbol of purity of heart and mind. A stunning temple, the Lotus Temple or Baha'i House of Worship, can be found in Delhi, India. It was designed in the shape of a half-opened lotus flower.

- The widest banyan tree in the world is located in Kolkata, India, and is approximately 250 years old. Banyan trees are planted near homes, temples, villages and roadsides as they provide welcome shade. In rural India, they are often the focal point of the village. Sap from the tree is used in external skin inflammations and bruising, and for treating toothaches and dysentery. A tonic made from parts of the tree is given to diabetic patients.

- Mango trees grow to 35–40 m in height with a crown radius of 10 m. Some mango trees are known to be as old as 300 years and still fruiting. India is the largest producer of mangoes in the world.

Answers

Answers will vary. An example of a Venn diagram with one abbreviated fact for each section is given below.

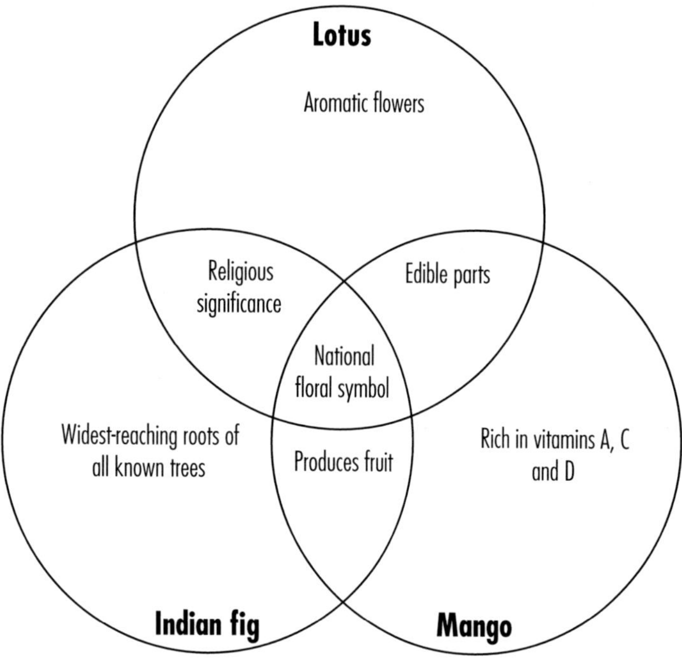

Additional activity

- Follow written or video instructions to make an origami lotus flower. If made with a pink or white serviette, the finished flower makes an attractive and practical table decoration. Useful websites are:

  <http://petalsofpeace.com/howto.htm>

  <http://www.origami-instructions.com/origami-lotus.html>

  <http://vodpod.com/watch/2100601-origami-lotus-instructions>

  The above websites were correct at the time of publication; however, teachers should check if links are still working and if content is correct.

National flora

The **national flower** of India is the **lotus**, an aquatic plant that grows in murky, shallow, still waters. It anchors in the mud below the surface and has long stems to which the leaves and flowers are attached. The leaves are shaped like discs and can be up to 90 cm in diameter. They can either float on the water or protrude well above it. The lotus has beautiful aromatic flowers with overlapping petals in hues of rosy-pink or white. The seeds, young leaves, stalks and flowers are all edible. Various parts are also used in herbal medicines.

The lotus is a sacred flower in the Hindu and Buddhist religions. It is significant for a number of reasons, including a symbol of wealth, fertility and knowledge; and for representing good fortune and long life.

The Indian fig (a type of **banyan** tree) is India's **national tree**. It is a huge structure with the widest-reaching roots of all known trees. It sprouts new shoots from its roots so it looks like a mass of branches, roots and trunks. Its large leaves are dark green and leathery. The Indian fig's fruit, which resembles reddish figs, is inedible. The tree acts as a useful shield from the hot sun. Parts of the tree are used to make things such as paper, rope, glue, toothpicks and medicinal items.

The widespread branches and roots of the tree symbolise India's unity as a nation. It is sacred to the Hindus of India and represents eternal life as it stretches out and appears to live for ever.

Described as the 'king of fruits', the **mango** is the **national fruit** of India. There are more than 100 varieties of mangoes in India, ranging in colours from green, yellow, red, orange and combinations of these. Size varies from 10 to 25 cm in length to 7 to 12 cm in width. It is savoured for its distinctive smell and sweet flavour. They are eaten ripe or prepared when green in pickles and are rich in vitamins A, C and D. Mangoes have been cultivated since ancient times in India.

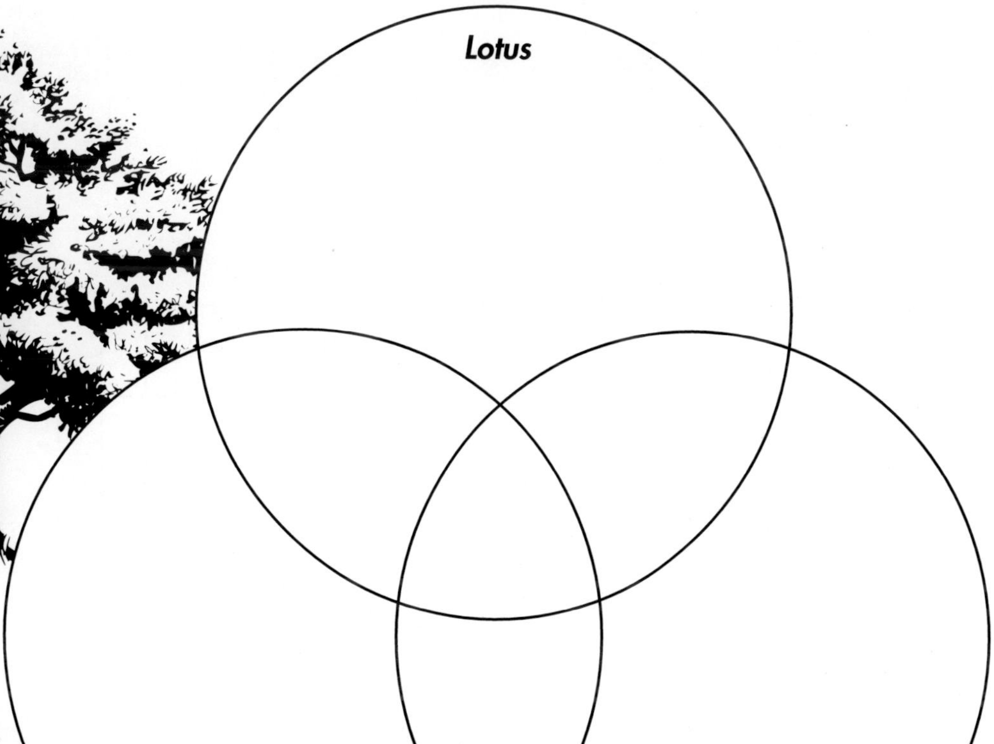

Highlight facts about each of the three national symbols above.

Use them to place at least one keyword or phrase in each section of the Venn diagram.

Lotus

Indian fig

Mango

Symbols

Objective

Reads information and completes a crossword puzzle.

Teacher information

- *Panthera tigris tigris*, known as the royal Bengal tiger, use to be found almost all over India, except in the north-west. A great number of them lived in the Sunderbans of Bengal; a forest of sunder trees. The male of this large cat, known as the 'king of the jungle' weighs about 200 kg and is about 3 metres long.

- The rare white tigers, also known as Bengal tigers, are not a subspecies nor albinos. They are white-coloured Bengals born to tigers that carry an unusual gene. They have blue eyes, a pink nose and chocolate stripes in their creamy white fur. Their light colour makes them highly visible to hunters so it is not surprising that most of them are now living in zoos or special wildlife parks.

- Pupils should be encouraged to discuss possible reasons why tigers are still hunted illegally in India and why local authorities are not always interested in supporting government efforts to preserve them in the wild and in the parks developed specifically for this purpose.

- The Indian elephant, *Elephas maximus indicus*, is one of three subspecies of the Asian elephant. They are adaptable and are found in a wide variety of habitats, including deserts and high mountain forests.

- Elephants are herbivores and rely on their molar teeth to grind their food. They cannot survive long without them. They need a huge amount of food but are only able to absorb a small proportion of it.

- As elephants in India and elsewhere are squeezed into smaller areas, they are becoming more aggressive and human-elephant conflict and violence is increasing. There have been reports of homes trampled and villagers killed by elephants seeking food, including rice stalks and moonshine brewed from rice. Some Indian villagers, unwilling to retaliate, have chosen instead to pray to Lord Garnesh, the remover of obstacles. Others have chased and moved the elephants on to other villages. But there have also been cases where large numbers of elephants have been deliberately poisoned. In Assam from 1990 to 2003, there were 586 human and 255 elephant victims of this conflict. It is an on-going problem.

Answers

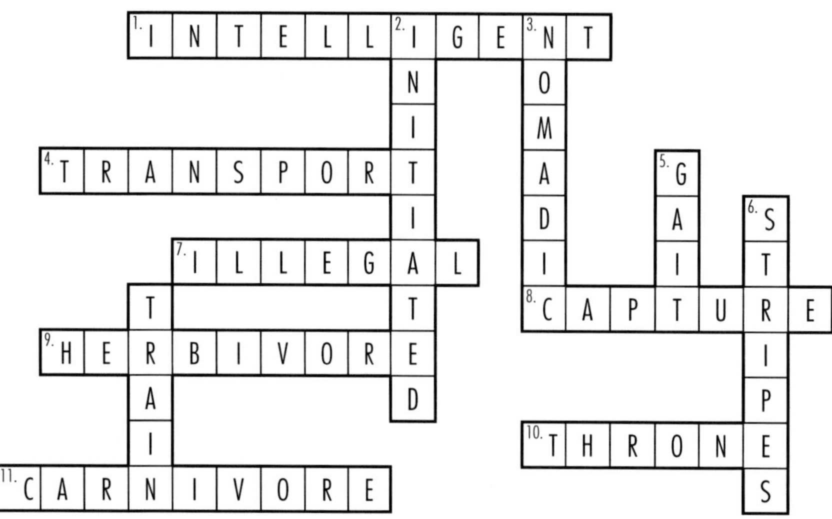

Additional activities

- Write an acrostic about India using the first letters of: Indian elephant.

- Write one sentence using as many words from the crossword as possible. Share the sentence with other class members and count the crossword words used. Then write a second sentence and try to improve on the first word count.

The Bengal tiger and Indian elephant

Although there are many magnificent animals found in India, the royal Bengal tiger's grace, strength, agility and enormous power made it the obvious choice for the country's national animal. The reddish-brown tiger with black stripes symbolises India's wonderful wildlife and it is held in high esteem by its people.

This richly-coloured animal is an excellent swimmer and has strong eyesight. It is a carnivore and a keen predator, eating deer, pigs, cattle, fish and occasionally humans. Many villagers try to protect themselves by offering prayers to the tiger.

In 1973, after tiger numbers were declining at such an alarming rate, a conservation programme was initiated. Considerable resources were committed to 'Project Tiger' and tiger numbers improved. However, despite the 27 tiger reserves set up, by 2009 the results were disappointing. Illegal smuggling and limited local support meant that on some of these reserves there wasn't even one tiger left.

Another wonderful example of India's wildlife is the world's largest land mammal, the Indian elephant. The Indian elephant is the biggest of the Asian elephants. Weighing 2.5–4.5 tonnes, it is considerably smaller than the African elephant (4–7 tonnes). Elephants are very highly regarded in India. Some Indians worship Lord Garnesh, the elephant god, who has an elephant's head and a human body.

Elephants are nomadic herbivores and need huge amounts of food and water. Their life span of about 60 years is determined by their teeth, which can only be replaced six times. They are highly intelligent, with excellent problem-solving skills, hearing and sense of smell, but with poor eyesight. They can run faster than a human but can't jump. They have great balance and can stand on two legs.

For more than 4000 years, the Asian elephant has been captured and trained. It has been used to lift and move heavy loads and as a means of transport. In the past, it was often the vehicle of choice for kings, who were carried in elaborately-decorated thrones. An elephant's slow and regal gait ensured a comfortable ride for the king and provided his subjects a clear view of their ruler.

Complete the crossword.

Across

1. Clever
4. Take from one place to another
7. Not legal
9. Take by force
10. A grass eater
11. Where a king sits
12. A meat eater

Down

2. Started
3. Wandering
5. A way of walking
6. Bands of different colours
8. To teach

Modern India

Objective

Reads, comprehends and completes information about urban living in present-day India.

Teacher information

- More information about cities in India can be found in the book *India* (Middle) on pages 9 and 36–39.
- Possible websites to aid pupils in their research to complete the table include:
  <http://www.world-gazetteer.com>
  <http://adaniel.tripod.com/cities.htm>
  <http://countrystudies.us/india/91.htm>.

Answers

Teacher check columns 4 and 5 as answers will vary. Some suggestions are provided as well as answers for columns 2 and 3. Pupils will find it easier to find answers for column 4 by researching to find information about the 'economy' of each city.

City	State/Territory	Approximate population	A major purpose or industry	An interesting fact
Mumbai	Maharashtra	13 922 125	Entertainment	'Bollywood' located here; Previously called Bombay
Delhi	National Capital Territory of Delhi	12 259 230	Information technology, retail	Second largest populated city in India
Bangalore	Karnataka	5 310 318	Colleges, research institutions, computer software	Known as 'the Silicon Valley of India'
Kolkata	West Bengal	5 080 519	Business, commerce	Former capital; previously called Calcutta
Chennai	Tamil Nadu	4 590 267	Automobiles, technology	Major centre for music, art and culture
Hyderabad	Andhra Pradesh	4 025 335	Information technology	Home of the world's largest film studio
Ahmedabad	Gujarat	3 913 793	Education, information technology, scientific industry	Centre of campaigns for workers and civil rights
Pune	Maharashtra	3 337 481	Education, manufacturing, glass, sugar, automobiles	The 2008 Commonwealth Youth Games were held here.
Jaipur	Rajasthan	3 102 808	Gas, tourism	Well-planned city; ranked the 7th best place to visit in Asia
Agra	Uttar Pradesh	1 638 209	Tourism, automobiles, leather, handicrafts	Location of the Taj Mahal

Additional activities

- Measure out 10 metres squared ($\frac{1}{100}$[th] of a square kilometre) and place 4 pupils in the space to demonstrate India's average population density. Repeat using 83 pupils for Delhi and 220 pupils for Mumbai. (The population density of Mumbai is estimated to be about 22 000 people per square kilometre!) Ask the pupils to imagine living in just that amount of space ALL the time. Discuss what essential items for survival would be needed to fill the space—sleeping area, cooking and eating area etc. (Remind pupils that bathing and toilet facilities may have been in the river and the streets.) Use a sheet of grid paper and an appropriate scale to draw or cut and paste shapes to represent furniture etc. to create a plan of a 'house' for a poor family in India. Compare to your own house plan, furniture and garden space.
- Complete a chart comparing rural and urban living.
- Reread the story of 'The town mouse and the country mouse' then write a new version including aspects of Indian lifestyle instead of the more familiar 'Western' version.

urban living

1. Read the text.

Despite the fact that only about 25% of the total population of India lives in urban areas, the number of people living in cities is rapidly increasing due to rural-to-urban migration.

Most cities in India are noisy, densely populated, extremely polluted and suffer from shortages of basic facilities such as adequate housing, sewerage, power, water supplies, schools and hospitals. The population density of India averages approximately 357 people per square kilometre. In Delhi in 2009, this figure is approximately 8261 people per square kilometre. Congested roads filled with a vast array of vehicles, pedestrians and animals create constant traffic jams, and a high rate of fatal accidents and injury. Uncontrolled pollutants from traffic and factories damage the urban environment.

Poverty is rife and extremes of wealth are very obvious. Wealthy houses complete with walled gardens, servants and garages sit alongside squalid slums rudely constructed from hessian and scrap timber.

Unemployment and underemployment are common for millions of urban dwellers. Relatives and friends assist where they can. However, increasing numbers of middle class urban dwellers, who work in offices, hospitals, courts and commerce, are emerging.

Indian cities are centres for commerce, finance, government, higher education, the computer and telecommunications industries and entertainment. Modern shopping centres, mills and factories sit adjacent to historical monuments, ancient religious architecture and busy tourist attractions.

2. Using any available resources complete the table below about these major cities.

City	State/Territory	Approximate population	A major purpose or industry	An interesting fact
Mumbai				
Delhi				
Bangalore				
Kolkata				
Chennai				
Hyderabad				
Ahmedabad				
Pune				
Jaipur				
Agra				

Rural living .... page 39

Objective

Reads and comprehends information about rural living in India.

Teacher information

- Farming in Indian villages is said to form the backbone of the entire Indian economy.

- Other agricultural products include milk, cashews, ginger, turmeric and mangoes. India is the world's largest producer of these.

- Agriculture in India operates in a number of different ways. Many farmers independently cultivate their crops on their own land. They may employ labourers/farmers to work the land with them occasionally, and contract farmers are employed to care for the land for the owner. Contract farmers do not own any of the land but are rewarded with a percentage of the crops as payment. Organic farming is becoming more popular, with practices such as crop rotation, animal by-products and mechanical cultivation used to maintain soil productivity and quality farmland.

- The languages spoken in villages vary greatly and create the major difference among them. Languages in different areas include Bengali, Punjabi, Tamil and Hindi, with the original, ancient forms of these languages usually found only in villages.

- In villages, the *panchayat* (council composed of important men from the major castes) traditionally settled disputes, only occasionally involving the police or judicial system. However, in modern India the government encourages an elected *panchayat* with a head person. The council now may include both women and members from the lower castes.

- Cottage industries such as the production of handicraft items, and the marketing of these, are a major occupation in rural India. Women are actively involved. Many villages have become famous for their particular handicrafts. Tourism is also becoming an important industry. Technology has also influenced the traditional occupations on farms, forcing villagers to take up other employment. A decline in land fertility from constant use is another factor influencing changing occupations.

- Fishing has been a major source of income in villages along the coast for centuries. Fish caught in rivers and the ocean — including mackerel, sardines, shark, ray, perch, sole, tuna, prawns, cuttlefish, carp, catfish and millet — are sold in the markets and overseas as a major export of India.

Answers

Answers will vary. Group discussion may facilitate a number of ideas before pupils work independently. Some suggestions for reasons for conflict, rivalry and self-interest groups may include: living in close proximity and having close relationships for many generations, problems involved in securing a basic living in an area with limited land and water resources, inequality between the wealthy and the poor, influence from the 'outside world' as villagers travel to cities to work, differences in education, the influence of television, increasing government influence.

Additional activities

- Pupils investigate and compare a rural area close to them to those in the text.

- Survey, tally and present a graph of occupations by categories for the parents of class members. Complete a summary stating whether any of these occupations are family-related or location-related occupations, or other categories.

Rural living

1. Read the fast facts about rural living in India.

The greater portion of the total population of India live in villages, of which there are about 550 000.

Village dwellings can be mud huts with thatched roofs or stone houses with tiled roofs.

The dwellings are often close together, with the village having narrow lanes for people, animals, cars and carts to pass through. Fields surround the settlement.

Villagers share common facilities such as the village pond ('the tank'), grazing areas, temples, shrines, cremation areas, schools and shady areas under trees for relaxing.

Traditionally, many villages recognise their own deity who protects their village.

Interdependence can unite villagers.

The Census* of India *considers settlements of fewer than 5000 people a village. Most villages are small, having less than 1000 inhabitants.*

*The Census of India *is a national census (an official counting of inhabitants, with details as to age, gender, pursuits etc.) performed every ten years.*

Each village connects to other villages close by as well as urban areas.

Usually a village is controlled by only one or a few caste(s). A headman (or men) from this/ these caste(s), is treated with great respect and as a source of advice. The council and the headman have the power to fine villagers or exclude them from social activities.

The main occupation in Indian villages is agriculture or occupations relating to agriculture. Products such as wheat, rice, lentils, vegetables and fruit feed the village and the country.

Languages spoken in villages differ among regions.

Most villages contain many groups which have different ways to provide for their families, are of different castes, and have difficult kinships, occupations and religions.

Many of India's traditional cultural forms, such as dance, music and puppetry, are popular in rural areas.

Villages near cities often have residents who travel there to work.

Other village occupations include priests; carpenters; blacksmiths; water bearers; leather workers; those who create handicrafts from wood, metal and leather; and weavers and potters.

Conflicts, rivalries and groups looking after their own interests arise in villages.

2. On the back of the worksheet or on a separate sheet of paper, create two columns—one headed 'Interdependence can unite villagers.' and the other 'Conflicts, rivalries and groups looking after their own interests arise in villages.' Write bullet points to suggest reasons to support each of these statements.

3. Use any descriptions included in the fast facts to sketch a village scene on a sheet of A3 art paper. You can use pencil or crayon and then colour it. When completed, compare it for accuracy to illustrations or photographs from other sources.

Modern India

Objective

Writes a magazine article describing the traditional clothing worn at a celebrity event.

Teacher information

- The many regions of India have developed their own distinctive brand of traditional clothing based on the climate and the natural fibres that have been readily available to them.

- For the general public, Western fashion styles for men are very common throughout India; for example, a business suit with shirt and tie or jeans and a casual shirt. Although the dhoti and lungi are worn on their own in tropical areas where trousers would be too uncomfortable, traditional clothing is often worn for special occasions only. The elegance of traditional menswear is highlighted with heavy embroidery and the wearing of gold jewellery.

- As in other countries of the world, the fashion industry in India is booming with a number of international fashion houses opening outlets.

Answers

Teacher check

Additional activities

- Design a poster to show how to tie a turban as worn by men in the Sikh community. Demonstrate the procedure to an audience.

- After class discussion, present ideas in a table outlining advantages and disadvantages of wearing traditional, Indian style and Western-style clothing.

Traditional men's clothing

Even in rural areas, men are more likely to be seen wearing Western-style clothes—but traditional outfits are still worn, particularly for special occasions.

Garments would originally have been made from natural materials like cotton or silk but now synthetic materials are also used. Rich fabrics and embroidery are used to create a stylish look for men's formal jackets. A scarf or shawl (called as **angavastram**) made from the same fabric is often carried as an accessory.

***Dhoti-kurta* – *Dhoti*:** a length of unstitched fabric about five metres long, wrapped around the waist and between the legs and then knotted at the waist.
***Kurta*:** a long loose-fitting shirt

Jodhpuri suit – elegant jacket with mandarin colour and gold embroidery, worn with Western-style trousers made from the same fabric.

Sherwani – a tailored, fitted coat, fastened in the front with buttons. Worn over a **churidar** (tight-fitting trousers), **salwar** (loose-fitting trousers) or dhoti.

Lungi – a length of fabric sewn into a circle (like a skirt) and fastened by rolling and knotting at the waist.

Write an article for a men's fashion magazine, describing the traditional clothes worn by the men at a celebrity event in Mumbai.

Modern India

Objective

Writes and presents a commentary script for a fashion show of traditional Indian clothing.

Teacher information

- *Sari* is a Sanskrit word meaning 'cloth'. It is an unstitched garment, ready to wear straight from the loom. The ancient Indians knew how to sew but unstitched cloth was considered pure. Tailored garments were introduced at the time of the Muslim invasions. A sari can be wrapped in different ways as required. It can be worn as a dress or, for working women, tied through the legs.

- It is thought that the choli was introduced by the British, for whom the elegant sari was an attractive addition to a woman's wardrobe. At about this time it became known in the fashion houses of Europe.

- The end of a sari can double up as a dupatta, but as a lehenga it is a separate skirt. A dupatta is can be used for any occasion when a woman's head must be covered.

- The kameez can vary in length and the sleeves, collar and fitting are altered as required.

- The loose-fitting salwar is brought into a collar at the ankles.

- The sharara is similar to the lehenga, but it is divided to the knee and flared from the knee to the floor. A red sharara is favoured by many Muslim women as a wedding dress.

Answers

Teacher check

Additional activities

- Collect a selection of clothes from home and adapt these to use in a presentation of glamorous traditional Indian clothing at a fashion show for the class.

- Research the Islamic concept of purdah and the garments associated with it—jilbabs, abas, hijabs and niqabs. Design an illustrated and informative poster to explain the idea and the different garments.

Traditional women's clothing

Although some women in India do wear Western clothes, traditional fashion is still more common, especially in rural areas. The different garments would originally have been made from natural materials like silk and cotton, but now many synthetic materials are also used.

Delicate material, patterning, embroidery, sequins and jewellery can be used to transform the basic design of an outfit from simple to glamorous.

Sari – a length of fabric 1 metre wide by about 4–9 metres long. Using a special technique, the fabric is wrapped around the body and tucked inside a **pavada** (petticoat), with the end of the fabric thrown over the left shoulder. A sari is sometimes worn with a **choli** (crop top).

Lehenga-choli – a combination outfit of a lehenga (long, swirling skirt) and choli, worn with a **dupatta** (shawl). A lehenga-choli is a popular wedding outfit.

Salwar kameez – a combination outfit of salwar (long, loose-fitting trousers) and a kameez (long, loose-fitting tunic) worn with a dupatta.

Churidar salwar-kameez – a combination of churidar (tight-fitting, extra long trousers) with the excess fabric gathering at the ankles, a kameez and dupatta.

Write the commentary script for a fashion show of glamorous traditional clothing. Add detailed descriptions of the fabric, colours and patterns as well as accessories worn by the models.

Objective

Completes a wordsearch using words related to savoury Indian cuisine.

Teacher information

- India covers a large area and includes a range of climates and soils, giving rise to great variety in the food and spices grown. Combine this with the cultures and traditions of the different regions and it is no surprise that 'Indian cuisine' is an exciting mixture of styles and flavour. Generally, the further south, the hotter the food.

- Since the days of the spice trade, Indian cuisine, with its characteristic blend of herbs, spices and different cooking oils, has influenced and been influenced by the cooking styles of the rest of the world.

- The commonly-known Indian cuisine regions are:

  - **northern Indian:** Punjabi, Mughlai and Bihari

  - **eastern India:** Bengali and Oriya

  - **southern India:** Andhra, Tamil and Karnataka

  - **western India:** Goan, Saraswati and Maharashtrian

Answers

L	O	Y	R	R	U	C	X	Z	T	C	Z	I	I
R	Y	J	D	F	T	H	T	B	D	D	N	R	M
C	N	L	G	O	Z	N	V	H	A	I	O	V	U
O	P	H	A	H	G	O	Z	H	E	O	D	E	S
C	U	M	G	O	G	U	K	T	D	S	H	G	T
O	L	V	A	L	C	N	O	N	Y	A	W	E	A
N	S	G	R	H	K	R	A	H	R	E	J	T	R
U	E	N	A	A	P	T	A	O	Z	P	S	A	D
T	S	F	E	D	P	S	T	H	J	T	N	B	P
C	S	A	I	F	L	I	X	G	C	I	A	L	K
R	O	T	K	I	S	S	E	A	N	L	E	E	U
O	V	N	T	K	E	F	U	G	M	P	B	S	W
N	G	N	Q	C	I	O	N	O	E	S	B	D	M
X	E	Y	I	S	F	T	X	I	B	U	J	M	C
L	K	P	H	E	N	A	A	N	R	I	C	E	M
Y	S	S	T	Z	V	V	I	N	D	A	L	O	O

Additional activities

- Plan and present a decorative menu for a special Indian meal.

- Design a poster with a map of India at its centre. Around the border, add pictures of regional dishes and link each to the map with string.

Savoury foods

To many people, Indian food is just about **curry**, a word that actually means 'sauce'. But just as there are many different sauces in international cuisine, so there are many different curries in India.

Most common in the north of the country, **tandoori** foods are cooked in a tandoor oven. This is a deep, cylindrical clay oven with a **charcoal** or wood fire burning at its base. Tandoori chicken and chicken **tikka** are well-known recipes cooked by this method. In the north, breads are a more popular accompaniment than rice. The dough of **roti** and **naan** breads are stuck to the hot sides of the tandoor oven and when they are baked, they fall away easily.

The Hindu religion proclaims that animals have souls and nonviolence to animals is widely recognised. So the staple foods of most Indians are **vegetables**, **pulses** and **rice**. They use pulses (**beans**, **lentils**, **split peas**) to make **dahl**, which is a thick tasty mixture, flavoured with **spices**, that is very high in **protein**.

In the east of the country where there are many rivers, **fish** is very plentiful and this is reflected in the local recipes. Cooking in **mustard** oil gives the fish a delicate, sweet flavour.

Recipes from Goa are famous for being hot and spicy, and slow-cooked in **coconut** milk for extra tenderness. They include the most famous of all Indian curries, the **vindaloo**.

Find all of the highlighted words in the puzzle.

L	O	Y	R	R	U	C	X	Z	T	C	Z	I	I
R	Y	J	D	F	T	H	T	B	D	D	N	R	M
C	N	L	G	O	Z	N	V	H	A	I	O	V	U
O	P	H	A	H	G	O	Z	H	E	O	D	E	S
C	U	M	G	O	G	U	K	T	D	S	H	G	T
O	L	V	A	L	C	N	O	N	Y	A	W	E	A
N	S	G	R	H	K	R	A	H	R	E	J	T	R
U	E	N	A	A	P	T	A	O	Z	P	S	A	D
T	S	F	E	D	P	S	T	H	J	T	N	B	P
C	S	A	I	F	L	I	X	G	C	I	A	L	K
R	O	T	K	I	S	S	E	A	N	L	E	E	U
O	V	N	T	K	E	F	U	G	M	P	B	S	W
N	G	N	Q	C	I	O	N	O	E	S	B	D	M
X	E	Y	I	S	F	T	X	I	B	U	J	M	C
L	K	P	H	E	N	A	A	N	R	I	C	E	M
Y	S	S	T	Z	V	V	I	N	D	A	L	O	O

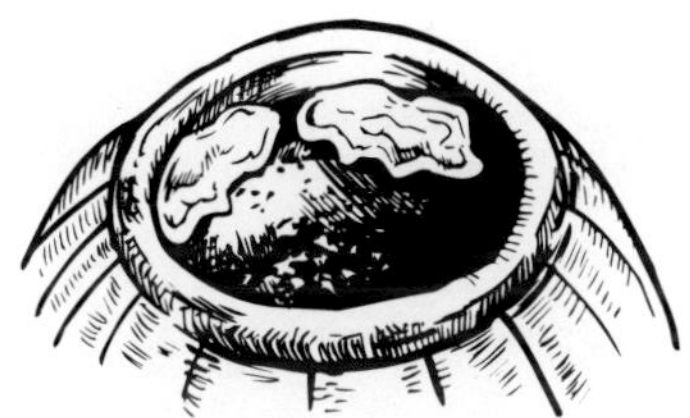

naan baking in a tandoor

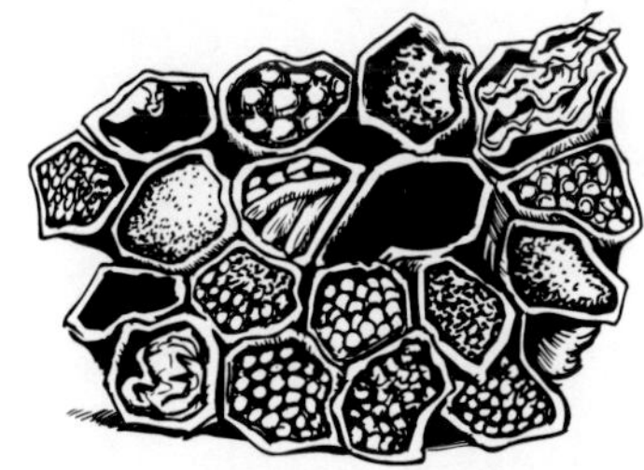

spices and pulses for sale in baskets

vindaloo

Modern India

Objective

Follows a procedure to make a traditional Indian dessert.

Teacher information

- India offers a wide variety of desserts known as *mithai*. They are very sweet and generally consumed to aid digestion after a spicy meal. Some are common throughout the subcontinent, while others are regional and may be typical of one area only. Like all Indian cuisine, the range of desserts has been influenced by the many cultures that have blended with Indian culture throughout its history. Generally, Indian desserts are either milk-based (such as rasbhari, peda and burfi) or flour-based (such as lal mohan, malpuwa and halva). Kulfi is a popular Indian ice-cream available in Indian restaurants throughout the world.

- Dried and fresh fruits and nuts are common ingredients for flavouring desserts.

Answers

Teacher check

Additional activities

- Prepare an Indian dessert menu, giving a brief description of a selection of different mithai.

- Design a poster with a map of India at its centre. Around the border, add pictures of regional desserts and link each to the map with string.

Sweet foods

In contrast to its spicy savoury cuisine, India is also famed for its sweet desserts known as 'mithai'.

Plain barfi is made by heating condensed milk with sugar until it solidifies. The name comes from 'baraf', the Hindi word for snow. Barfi is often flavoured to make it even more delicious. Additions include cashew or pistachio nuts, mango or figs or a choice of spices.

For a special effect, barfi can be topped with a thin layer of varak, or edible silver leaf. As it looks similar to a soft cheese, barfi is often referred to as 'Indian cheesecake'.

1. Follow the procedure to make a delicious coconut barfi.

Ingredients

400 g condensed milk

300 g grated coconut

100 g full-cream milk powder

½ cup whole milk

1 sheet varak (optional)

Method

- Line a lamington tray with greased baking paper.
- Add condensed milk, grated coconut, milk powder and milk to a thick-bottomed pan.
- Over a medium heat, stir constantly until the mixture begins to bubble.
- Reduce heat and continue to stir until the mixture leaves the sides of the pan.
- Roll to fit a lamington tray.
- Peel the sheet of varak and press on to barfi.
- Allow it to cool.
- Cut barfi into squares and serve.

2. Under each heading, write words to describe the coconut barfi.

Look	Taste	Texture	Smell

3. Give your coconut barfi a rating.

(a) taste   *unpleasant* ☆ ☆ ☆ ☆ ☆ *delicious*

(b) baking   **difficult** ☆ ☆ ☆ ☆ ☆ **easy**

Modern India

Objective

Reads information and answers questions about the education system in India.

Teacher information

- The education system in India is divided into primary, secondary (or intermediate), senior secondary (or high school), and higher education. Primary school consists of grades one to five (ages six to 11), middle school is grades six to eight (pupils aged 11 to 14) and high school consists of grades nine to 12 (ages 14 to 17). Higher education provides pupils with an opportunity to specialise in a field and includes technical schools, colleges and universities.

- India's literacy rate has been increasing since independence and is currently around 61%. Female literacy is at a national average of around 48%, whereas male literacy is closer to 75%. There are far fewer girls enrolled in schools, and many of those that do attend schooling drop out early. Barriers to female education include inadequate school facilities (such as sanitary facilities), shortage of female teachers, and many girls, especially in rural areas, being required to stay at home and perform domestic duties. UNICEF reports that of India's 700 000 rural schools, only one in six have toilets, deterring children from attending and completing schooling. Rural areas have fewer schools and a lower attendance than urban areas.

- The government has a number of incentive programmes in progress to encourage children to attend school, such as the Midday Meal Scheme, which involves provision of lunch free of charge to schoolchildren on all working days.

- Many schools are overcrowded in India, with pupil-teacher ratios of up to 80:1.

Answers

1. Teacher check

2. Answers will vary. Larger class sizes might result in less access to resources, less individual attention and assistance from teachers, less accommodation for diversity, and possibly more distractions resulting from noise levels, behaviour and discipline.

3. Teacher check

Additional activities

- Divide pupils into small groups. Each group chooses a different state of India. They research to find the literacy rate in that state and what physical or other factors affect the rate. Groups can add their findings to a class bar graph, or present their findings as a presentation.

- Use the Internet to find a picture of a rural classroom (preferably where pupils are sitting on the floor to learn) in India to show to the pupils. (An example can be found at <http://en.wikipedia.org/wiki/File:Girls_in_school_Gujarat.jpg>.) The pupils then write a short story about what it might be like to go to such a school.

Education

1. Read the information.

Early in India's history, education was only available to people from certain social classes (castes). The Brahmin caste learned about religion, the Kshatriya were educated in warfare and the Vaishya learned commerce.

Knowledge was mostly passed on orally by spiritual leaders and teachers called gurus. Members of the lower castes did not have access to education. Instead boys from these castes learned their family trade from their fathers.

Today, the Indian government provides free education for all Indian children from ages six to 14. However, despite the fact that primary and middle schooling is compulsory, around 8 million children do not attend primary school. One reason for this is that, because many families are extremely poor, they send their children to work. Although child labour has been banned, millions of children between the ages of 5–14 years work in India. This is especially a problem in rural areas, where, enrolment in primary and middle schools is very low and a large percentage of children leave school before the fifth grade. Many are girls, whose parents force them to stay home and perform household chores. This is one reason the percentage of illiterate (cannot read or write) females in India is much higher than that of males. Another factor affecting education is a lack of teachers, especially in rural and mountainous areas. Many primary school classes in India have around 40 pupils per teacher.

India's education system comprises of primary education (eight years), secondary education (two years), senior secondary education (two years) and higher education. There are both private and government schools available.

2. Under the headings in the chart, briefly describe how having 40 pupils in your class might affect your ability to learn.

Access to resources (books, computers)	Time spent with teacher	Noise levels and disruptions

3. Write two ways in which education in India is similar to that in your country, and two ways it is different. (Continue on the back of this sheet, if necessary.)

____

____

____

____

Modern India

Objective

Reads information and answers questions about transport in India.

Teacher information

- In India today, there is a wide variety of modes of transport by land, water and air. A small percentage of Indians own their own vehicles—around 10% of households own a motorcycle and around 1% own a car. Public transport is the primary mode of transport for most of the population.

- India's rail network is one of the longest and most heavily used system in the world. Indian Railways carries around 14 million passengers a day.

- India has 12 major ports along its coastline that serve the country's foreign trade of resources and products. Growing international trade is putting strain on these ports.

- The text on the pupil's page focuses on road transport, as use of roads is the dominant mode of transportation in India.

Answers

2. (a) Bullock carts   (b) Buses   (c) palanquin   (d) Cycle rickshaws
   (e) auto rickshaw   (f) Vans and minibuses   (g) Metro (underground train)   (h) air travel

3. palanquin, cycle rickshaw, auto rickshaw/fat-fat.

Additional activities

- Explain how advancements in transport technology could affect communication, nutrition, health care and agriculture in the remote or rural areas of India.

- The decoration of a palanquin reflected the status of its owner. Enlarge the image of the palanquin on page 51 for pupils to colour or decorate to reflect themselves.

- Give small groups of pupils the names of two cities in India. They find where they are on a map, then list the different ways a person could travel between the two cities.

Transport

1. Read the descriptions of some of the types of transport used for travel in India today.

Metro (underground train)   Buses   auto rickshaw
Bullock carts   palanquin
Vans and minibuses   Air travel   Cycle rickshaws

2. Match the name of each kind of transport to its description below.

(a) _________________________ are a common means of transportation and have been used since ancient times in India. They are still used today when modern vehicles are too expensive or roads are poor. They are often used to transport agricultural goods to markets.

(b) _________________________ are a cheap and easy mode of transport used by many Indians for both short and long distance road travel. In the big cities and towns of India, these are the major mode of transport, and they also connect major cities and towns.

(c) A _________________________ is a covered litter for a person carried on poles. They were originally used by the wealthy, especially noble women, who were carried inside by men holding the poles. They are today sometimes used by tourists, or brides for Hindu wedding celebrations.

(d) _________________________ are a three-wheeled, pedal-powered mode of transport, with seats in the back to seat passengers and a 'driver' in the front.

(e) An _________________________ is a three wheeled vehicle (one wheel in front, two on the rear), usually without doors or seatbelts, available for hire. They are generally yellow or green with a black or green canopy on the top. Up to three paying passengers can be seated in the rear. A fat-fat is a larger version, carrying as many as ten paying passengers.

(f) _________________________ offer a taxi-like service allowing the large percentage of the population without cars to travel short to medium distances, especially in remote areas.

(g) _________________________ systems can be found in larger cities like Mumbai, Kolkata, Chennai and Delhi. India also has an extensive above-ground rail network, one of the longest in the world. Farmers use this national network to transport their produce to towns across India.

(h) _________________________ is becoming more affordable in India. Many airlines connect more than 80 cities across India and internationally.

3. Label these forms of transport described in the text above.

_________________________   _________________________   _________________________

Modern India

Objective

Designs a poster promoting India as a modern industrialised nation.

Teacher information

- India has a massive population and, therefore, a huge workforce. The country is working to improve its position in the global economy.
- Since independence, various strategies and incentives have been introduced by governments in India to improve its economy and position in the global market. These include:
  - investing in new industries and embracing new technologies
  - developing modern production and management techniques for running businesses
  - government support of younger entrepreneurs
  - creating industrial centres throughout the country
  - investing to provide and improve domestic and commercial infrastructure, including power, communication and transport
  - encouraging traditional industries with financial support and incentives.
- Until the early 1960s, India had to import food to feed its rapidly expanding population. A series of government-led policies, now known as the 'Green Revolution', sought to improve the agricultural industry and make the country self-sufficient. Today, the country produces more food than it needs, the rest being exported.

Answers

Teacher check

Additional activities

- Draft a human resource chain for any industry to show the many levels of production used in creating a finished product from its raw materials. Use the draft to create an illustrated poster.
- Research to draw two pie charts showing the major industries in India: one chart showing the percentage of people employed in each industry, the other showing the income each industry creates.

Industry

Since independence, successive Indian governments have strived to develop different industries and create many job opportunities in order for India to become a prosperous, modern nation with a sound industrial base.

Agriculture has always been India's largest industry and it leads the world in the production of some foods such as milk, bananas, coconuts and some spices.

The success of any year's harvest has always been affected by the monsoons. In recent years, the government has introduced irrigation and draining methods to counteract damage done by heavy rains during the monsoon season.

The textile industry is the second largest industry in the country. Many people are employed at the different levels of production, including providing raw materials, weaving fabrics, designing and making garments, and packaging, transporting and selling the finished products.

Traditional Indian crafts are a major source of income in rural areas. They are in great demand from Western tourists and for exporting to Western countries. Popular items include hand-knotted carpets, hand-printed textiles and leather and cane ware.

The Indian railway system is one of the largest in the world. At over 63 thousand kilometres in length, it carries over 6 billion passengers and 728 million tonnes of freight each year.

Most of the motorised vehicles that travel on the massive network of roads across the country are made in India as many foreign motor companies have established manufacturing plants there.

Coal, petroleum and natural gas are the major sources of energy across India, with the country having the resources to satisfy its own demand.

Almost one hundred countries across the globe use information technology and services located in India. Many companies worldwide outsource their remote maintenance, accounting and call centres from India. This has given the Indian economy an enormous boost which is set to increase for years to come.

Many multinational companies have invested in the Indian market, opening offices and factories in major cities. This shows their faith in India as an industrialised nation with the potential for an even stronger economy. Also, Indian companies have gained recognition worldwide and are trading in the international market.

**Use the information from the text to design a poster
promoting India as a modern industrialised nation.**

Modern India

Objective

Reads and comprehends information about Indian currency.

Teacher information

- On 5 March 2009, the Indian Government announced a public competition to design an official symbol for the Indian national Rupee.
- Although the coins commonly in circulation today are the 10, 25 and 50 paise and 1, 2 and 5 rupees, the 1, 2, 3 and 20 paise coins are still in existence but rarely used on a regular basis.
- In September 2009, the Reserve Bank of India introduced Rs 10 polymer banknotes on a trial basis. These will have an average life span of five years (four times that of the current paper banknotes), be cleaner and be more difficult to counterfeit.
- The obverse is the side of the coin or banknote which bears the head or principal design. The opposite of obverse is reverse.
- Each current Indian rupee banknote gives the denomination of the note in 7 of the 22 official languages of India.
- The security features on the banknotes include: a watermark, a security thread, a latent image of the note's value in numerals when held horizontally at eye level, microlettering, fluorescent number panels, optically variable ink, back-to-back registration and the Eurion constellation (a pattern of symbols [five rings]).

Answers

1. Teacher check

2.

Note value	Main colour	Image on obverse	Image on reverse	Date of issue
Rs 5	green	Mahatma Gandhi	tractor	2002
Rs 10	orange–violet	Mahatma Gandhi	rhinoceros, elephant and tiger	1996
Rs 20	red–orange	Mahatma Gandhi	palm trees	2002
Rs 50	violet	Mahatma Gandhi	Parliament of India	1997
Rs 100	blue–green in the centre and brown–purple at two sides	Mahatma Gandhi	Himalaya Mountains	1996
Rs 500	olive–green	Mahatma Gandhi	the Dandi march	1997
Rs 1000	amber–red	Mahatma Gandhi	Economy of India	2000

Additional activities

- Access the full details of the competition from the Indian Ministry of Finance and hold your own class competition to create a global symbol for the rupee by following the rules.
- Check the current exchange rate and convert the cost of common items such as an apple, pen, CD, hamburger, can of soft drink etc. to rupees.

Currency

1. Read the information about the currency of India.

The official (and original) currency of India is the Indian national rupee. It is most commonly represented by the symbols Rs and INR.

The word 'rupee' means 'silver'. Originally the rupee was a silver coin but with most countries around the world using gold as their standard and the discovery of vast quantities of silver in the US and European countries, the Indian silver coins lost much of their value. Over time, the various coins have changed, with some removed from circulation. The current coins are made from aluminium or stainless steel and the Rs 10 coin uses copper as well.

In 1861, when the British occupied India, the first paper banknotes were introduced; however, after independence, these were changed in 1949 to remove the image of the British king.

The units of Indian currency are the rupee and paisa. One hundred paisa equals one rupee. Paper money comes in denominations of 5, 10, 20, 50, 100, 500 and 1000 Rupee. The coins come in denominations of 10, 25 and 50 paisa and 1, 2 and 5 rupees.

2. The current series of notes in circulation, which were first issued in 1996, is called the Mahatma Gandhi series. The table below gives some details about them. Use any available resources to complete the missing details.

Note value	Main colour	Image on obverse	Image on reverse	Date of issue
Rs 5		Mahatma Gandhi		2002
Rs. 10			rhinoceros, elephant and tiger	
Rs 20				2002
Rs 50			Parliament of India	
Rs 100	blue–green in the centre and brown–purple at two sides			
Rs 500			the Dandi march	
Rs 1000			Economy of India	

Objective

Reads and completes information about sports in India.

Teacher information

- In ancient India, athletes competed in sports such as chariot racing, archery, horsemanship, wrestling, weightlifting, hunting, swimming and running races. A few traditional sports are still practised today but are not as popular as modern sports. Some modern sports may have evolved from more traditional ones.

- During the British Raj, many British sports (such as cricket, hockey, tennis and football) were introduced to the Indian people, while some Indian games (such as badminton) carried to other parts of the world.

- Traditional sports of India include kabaddi, gilli-danda and kho-kho (Refer to pages 26–27 of India [Middle] of this series and pages 20–22 of India [Lower] for further information) and thoda (a form of martial arts with an emphasis on archery expertise), silambam (a form of fencing) and pachisi (a board game in the shape of a cross).

- Indians play a variety of sports depending on their socioeconomic background and the region in which they live. More traditional sports are played by Indians as they are inexpensive.

Answers

The websites <http://www.iloveindia.com/sports/index.html> and <http://sports.indianetzone.com/> will provide assistance for pupils searching for the names of athletes for each sport listed. Some well-known players in the sports include:

- Hockey: Balbir Singh, Dhyan Chand, Suraj Lata Devi
- Cricket: Sachin Tendulkar, Kapil Dev
- Badminton: Saina Nehwal, Abhinn Shyam Gupta, Nikhil Kanetkar
- Shooting: Abhinav Bindra, Rajyavardhan Singh Rathore, Samaresh Jung
- Weightlifting: Geeta Rani, Yumnam Chanu, Kunjarani Devi
- Tennis: Sania Mirza, Leander Paes
- Table tennis: Achanta Sharath Kamal
- Football: Baichung Bhutia, Chuni Goswami

Additional activities

- Select one of the elite Indian athletes and write a biography about them including information about what inspired them to succeed in their chosen sport.

- Use an appropriate graph organiser to record information such as equipment needed, number of players, rules, safety regulations, uniforms etc. about the sports listed.

Sports

India has a rich history of involvement in sports. Indian athletes participate in the Olympic Games, the Commonwealth Games, the Asian Games, the South Asian Games, Wimbledon and many other world sporting tournaments.

Read about some of the sports, then write names of one or more elite sports people for each sport.

Hockey is the national sport of India. It is played widely by both men and women. Hockey was introduced by the British army during their occupation of India.

Combined, the men's and women's Indian hockey teams have won eight gold, one silver and two bronze medals at the Olympic Games, and one gold and one silver at the Commonwealth Games.

Cricket is the most popular game played in India. Also introduced by the British, the Indian cricket team has won success in the World Cup, one day and test matches. Many well-known Indian cricket players are respected around the world.

Cricket has also become a peaceful arena for India and Pakistan to settle political differences.

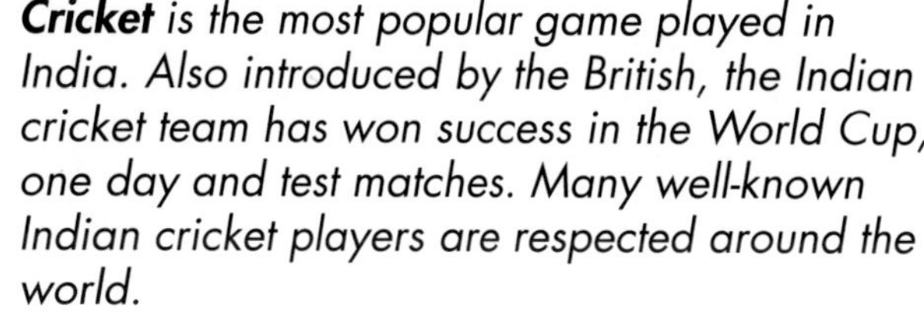

Badminton, which is believed to have originated in India, is a popular recreational sport. Despite limited international success, it continues to grow.

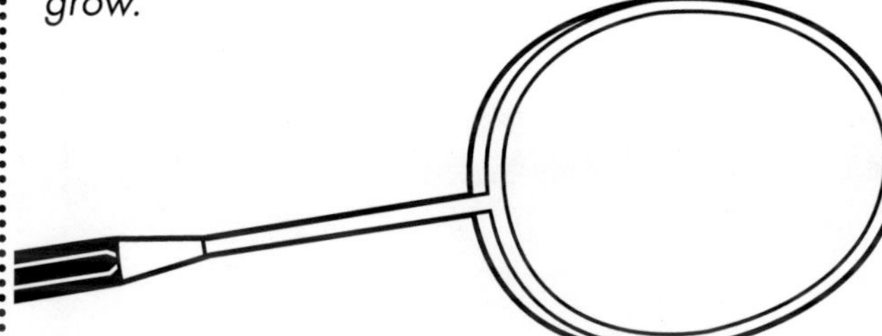

Shooting is popular primarily with wealthy Indians as it is an expensive sport which few can afford to compete in. Despite this, many Indian shooters have been successful in Olympic and Commonwealth Games competitions, winning gold and silver medals.

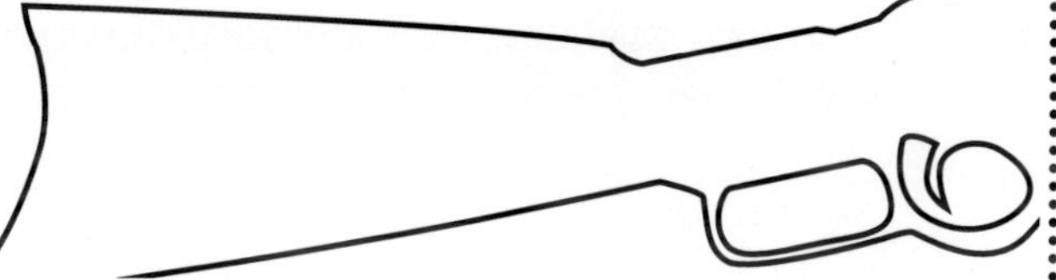

Weightlifting in India, popularly known as 'lifting', has increased in stature from its early beginnings, gaining modest success in the World Championships, Commonwealth Games and Olympic Games.

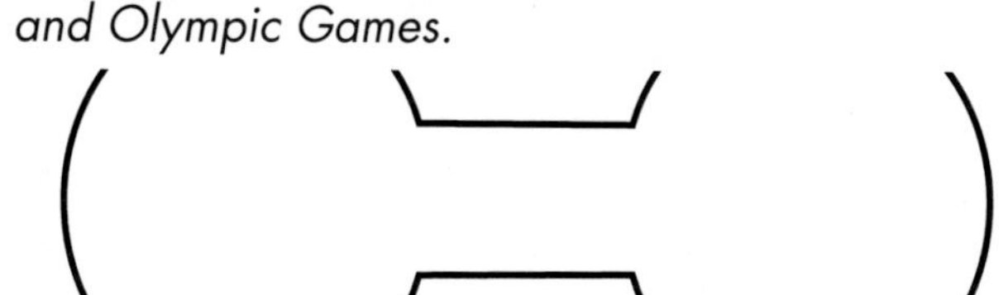

Like cricket and hockey, *tennis* was introduced by the British. Since the 1990s, it has increased in popularity due mainly to the international success of many of the elite players.

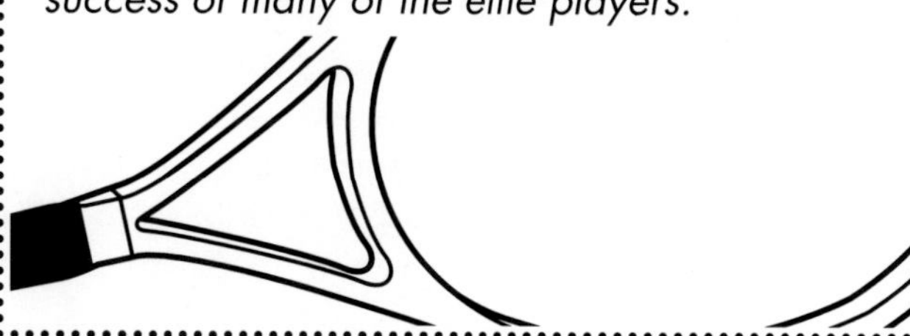

Although not as popular as cricket or tennis, **table tennis** is still played in India and has produced medal winners in teams and individual events at the Melbourne 2006 Commonwealth Games.

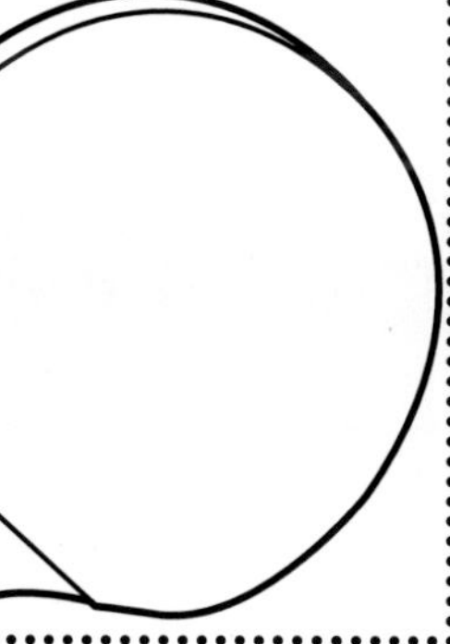

Football is a very important sport and, in some regions, as popular as cricket. Although less successful recently than in the past at the international level, football is still a major sport in India.

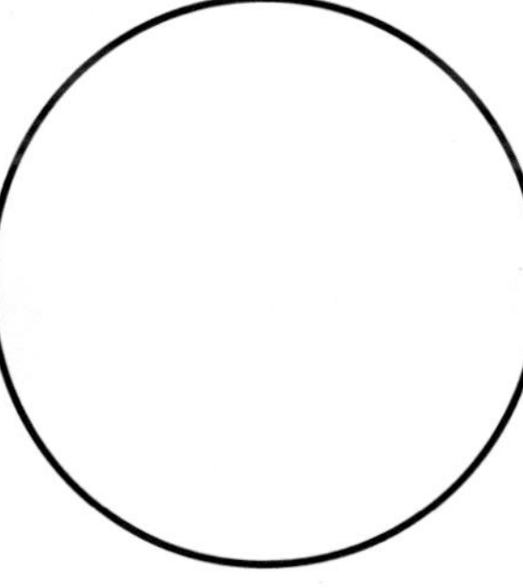

Modern India

The caste system..page 59

Objective

Reads, comprehends and completes information about the caste system of India.

Teacher information

- The concept of the caste system is quite complicated. The Western understanding of caste may differ greatly from that of the Hindus. It is considered to be a religious concept as well as a series of social groupings.

- There are many subcastes/communities (or *jati*) of each caste/varna, resulting in numerous diverse social groups. Estimates suggest that there may be thousands of subcastes.

- There are several different theories about how the caste system was established, many of which are controversial. These include the religious/mythological theory about Purusha; an unfounded biological theory which suggests that all living things inherit three qualities (such as intelligence, courage, and creativity) in different portions; and a social/historical theory that the caste system was established at some point during the first millennium BCE.

- According to religious beliefs, each varna had rules of purity. The Brahmins were the most pure so they would only eat food prepared by other Brahmins. If a Brahmin priest touched an 'untouchable', he had to perform rituals to wash away the impurities.

- Many Dalits lived on the outskirts of cities and villages and had to take water downstream from the other castes. They were not allowed to share wells with the other castes. It was believed that they deserved this treatment because of bad karma or because of something bad they may have done in a previous life.

- Hindus believe that they must work hard to live up to the rules and expectations of their jati or varna.

- The first three castes (Brahmins, Kshatriyas and Vaishyas) are considered to be 'twice born', having gone through a first natural birth and a second ceremonial or religious birth or entrance into society.

- People in a caste virtually 'inherited' their occupation from their parents as they were historically expected to go into the same profession according to their caste. However, new socioeconomic patterns have allowed lower castes the opportunity to improve their station in life by changing their employment status due to the availability of better educational opportunities and a growing awareness of the inequalities of the caste system.

Answers

1. Teacher check
2. Refer to graph. Pupils may wish to add additional bullet points about each caste to complete this question if they wish.
3. See triangle.

Additional activity

- Read about the life of Mahatma Gandhi (refer to pages 94 and 95). To find out about his efforts to change the situation of the Harijans/Dalits.

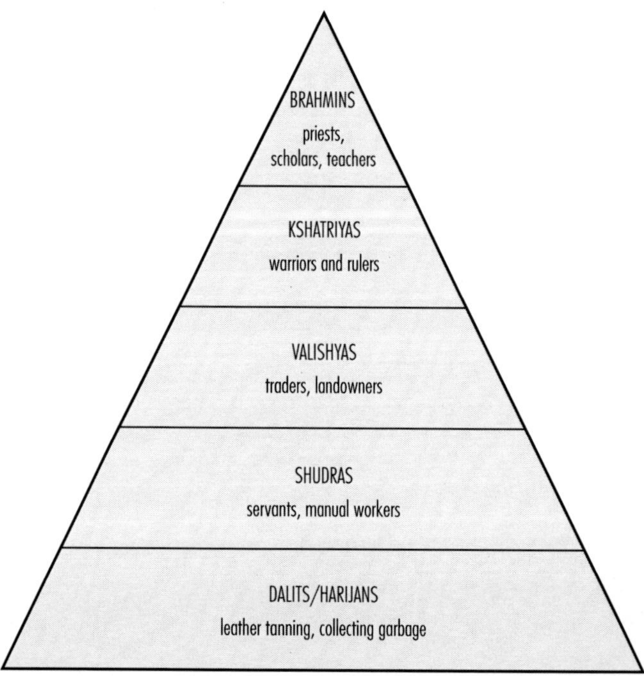

The caste system

According to Hindu mythology, the first man, Purusha, sacrificed himself in order to create the universe, and humans in particular. His body was torn into four different pieces from which different castes (or social groups) of people formed.

From Purusha's head came the most important group—the Brahmins, who became the priests, scholars and teachers. From his arms came the Kshatriyas—the warriors and rulers. From his thighs came the Valishyas (the traders and landowners), and from his feet came the Shudras, the servants and manual workers.

Those not included in these four groups were considered outcasts. This least important, and largest, group was called the Dalits or Harijans. Other castes did not associate with them and, for this reason, they were also called the 'Untouchables'. They did the least desirable jobs such as leather tanning or collecting garbage. The name 'Harijans', which translated means 'Children of God', was first given to them by Gandhi in an attempt to stop prejudice against them. The religious word for castes is 'varna'.

Traditionally, each caste was defined by its deeds, occupation, language, dress or eating habits. Caste was determined by birth—a person was born into a particular caste and was expected to marry and stay within it. To Hindus, the caste system provided a division of labour and explained how the universe worked.

The caste system remained unchanged for about two thousand years and, to some extent, still exists today. To many people, it is seen as unfair as it means that people are looked down on for no reason other than who their parents are. For this reason, the government of India is attempting to improve the situation of the lower castes by trying to create a truly democratic society where laws state that no person in any particular group should be discriminated against because of his or her caste. Other changes to the caste system have been the result of Western influences, modernisation, industrial developments and urbanisation.

1. Highlight keywords in each paragraph.

2. Complete the hierarchical organiser, including the name of each caste and the traditional occupation of each.

3. Order the castes from most to fewest by the amount of people in each. Use the hierarchical chart to help.

   Once completed, discuss with your classmates how fair or unfair you think the caste system is.

Government in India...page 61

Objectives

- Reads and comprehends information about the government of India.
- Completes a cryptogram relating to the government of India.

Teacher information

- India, a union of states, is known as 'Bharat' in the language of Hindi.
- The office of president of India is symbolic and procedural: The president is the supreme commander of the armed forces; appoints the prime minister, state governors and supreme court justices, and has the power to declare a state of emergency in case of threats to national security, or because of war or armed rebellion.
- The prime minister is the head of the 'Council of Ministers' and it is their job to assist and advise the president. The Council of Ministers is responsible to the Lok Sabha (the House of the People).
- The Rajya Sabha (the Council of States) is a permanent body made up of cabinet posts and ministers of states. It cannot be dissolved by the president. However, about one-third of its members retire after only two years of their six-year term and are replaced by newly-elected members. The chairman of Rajya Sabha is the vice president of India who is assisted by an elected deputy chairman. A panel of vice chairmen forms the remainder of the Rajya Sabha, with the most senior Minister appointed by the prime minister as 'Leader of the House'.
- The Lok Sabha (the House of the People) controls the money used to administrate the country. It can be dissolved by the president. Lok Sabha representatives are elected in ratio to each state's population. Representatives must be over 25 years of age. From the representatives, a speaker is chosen who is responsible for the organisation and administration of the Lok Sabha, business.
- In order for a bill to become law, both Lok Sabha and Rajya Sabha must pass the bill.
- The states have their own governors and elected representatives who are appointed by the president. Some states have an upper house or state legislative council. Each state's council of ministers advises that state's governor in carrying out his or her duties. The council of ministers of a state are directly responsible to the legislative assembly of the state.
- The Union territories are centrally administered by an administrator appointed by the president.
- Teachers may wish to ask pupils to underline or highlight words or phrases in each paragraph to aid their understanding of the concepts presented.

Answers

India is a sovereign, socialist, democratic republic.

Additional activities

- Use a graphic organiser to draw a diagram to explain the government of India.
- Visit the Indian Government website <http://india.gov.in/govt.php> to find out who the current heads of government are, and to read more details about parliament and India's constitution.

Government in India

Read the information then complete the cryptogram below.

The Republic of India, commonly known as India, is a sovereign country.

In terms of population, India is the largest democracy in the world. It is a republic with a parliamentary system of government.

India's constitution (system of principles by which a nation, state or body politic is governed) was set in place in 1950 after the country became independent from Britain. The parliament consists of the president and the two houses of parliament, with the president recognised as the official head of state.

The president is elected indirectly by an electoral college for a term of five years, but the prime minister exercises most executive powers. The Prime Minister is appointed by the president and is almost always the head of the majority party in the lower-house of parliament.

The bicameral federal parliament consists of an upper house called the Rajya Sabha (Council of States) and a lower house called the Lok Sabha (House of the People). The Rajya Sabha has 250 members who serve for six years. Most are elected by the governments of India's states and territories and up to another 12 are appointed by the President. The Lok Sabha has about 545 members who are elected by India's population for terms of five years.

The Constitution of India recognises three branches of government: the Executive (the president, prime minister, vice-president and Council of Ministers), the Legislature (the lower and upper houses), and the judiciary (the supreme court, headed by the Chief Justice; 21 high courts and many lower-level courts).

General elections are held every five years, with every adult over 18 years of age eligible to vote.

The federal government is in New Delhi, but there are 28 state governments and seven union territories.

Definitions:

- sovereign — a nation having authority over itself.

- socialism — a theory or system of social organisation which supports the administration by the government of the nation's economy.

- democracy — a form of government where the power is in the hands of the people and exercised by them or by their elected agents under a free electoral system.

- republic — a state, especially a democratic state, in which the head of the government is an elected or nominated president, not a hereditary monarch.

- bicameral — having two branches, chambers, or houses, as a legislative body.

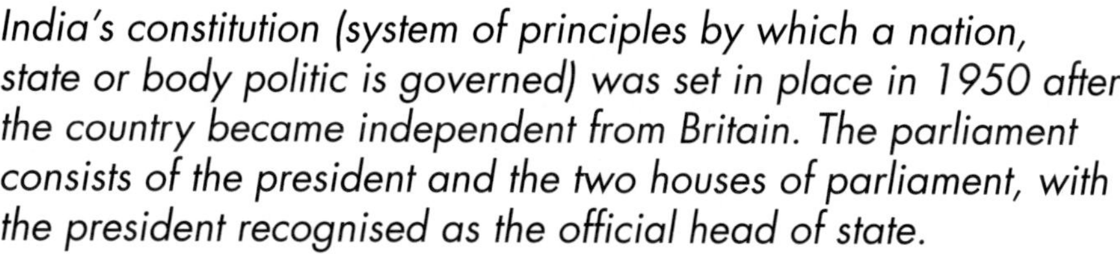

A	B	C	D	E	G	I	L	M	N	O	P	R	S	T	U	V
10	18	15	24	26	4	9	13	23	3	14	19	5	20	22	11	17

```
 __ __ __ __ __     __ __     __     __ __ __ __ __ __ __ __ __ ,     __ __ __ __ __ __ __ __ __ ,
  9  3 24  9 10      9 20     10     20 14 17 26  5 26  9  4  3      20 14 15  9 10 13  9 20 22

 __ __ __ __ __ __ __ __ __ __     __ __ __ __ __ __ __ __ __ __ .
 24 26 23 14 15  5 10 22  9 15      5 26 19 11 18 13  9 15
```

Religions, customs and celebrations

Objective

Completes activities about the religion of Islam in India.

Teacher information

- Although a number of religions are practised in India, Hinduism is by far the most dominant. The middle book of this series covers Hinduism on pages 62–65.

- The Islamic calendar is known as the Hijri calendar. The calendar is similar to the lunar year and is about 10 days shorter than the Gregorian calendar. The months gradually drift backwards over the seasons, taking about 33 years to reach the same starting point.

- Unhappy with his life in Mecca, Mohammed went to live in a cave in the mountains surrounding the city. Here he had time for meditation and reflection. It was at this place, in the month of Ramadan, that he received his first revelation from Allah (God).

- When he began preaching, Mohammed gained few followers and came into conflict with some Meccan tribes. To escape persecution, Mohammed and his followers migrated to Medina, in 622 CE. This migration, known as the Hijra, heralds the beginning of the Islamic calendar.

- After eight years of fighting with the Meccan tribes, Mohammed and his followers conquered Mecca. Mohammed died in 632, by which time most of the Arabian Peninsula had converted to Islam.

Answers

Page 64

Objective

Completes activities about the religion of Buddhism in India.

Teacher information

- Siddhattha Gautama was born into a wealthy Hindu family in Lumbini in present-day Nepal. Having lived a privileged life and being sheltered from the pain and suffering of the masses, he was shocked when, at the age of 29, he witnessed them for the first time. He left his luxurious home and took up a lifestyle of self-induced hardship and deprivation.

- In searching for a reason for the extremes of suffering and opulence, Siddhattha discovered the 'Middle Way', a road between self-denial and self-indulgence. This way took his mind off the stress of hunger and physical discomfort, allowing him to meditate freely. His experiences along this Middle Way brought him to enlightenment.

- As Buddha, he began teaching about enlightenment as something that can be achieved by everyone. The early Buddhists travelled across Asia, spreading the teachings of Buddha. Over time, Buddhism was interwoven with the traditional culture and customs of different regions resulting in variations of the Buddhist philosophy.

- The two branches of Buddhism are Theravada and Mahayana. Within Mahayana Buddhism are two further sub-groups: Tibetan and East Asian. East Asian is further divided into five groups. But in all these variations, the Dharma (the teachings of Buddha, which is the essence of the Buddhism) do not vary.

Answers

1.
(a) reincarnation (b) enlightenment (c) meditation
(d) nirvana (e) Tripitaka (f) Baskets
(g) Wisdom (h) Dharma (i) Sangha
(j) Three (k) Signs (l) Being
(m) Four (n) Noble (o) Truths
(p) Noble (q) Eightfold (r) Path
(s) Wheel (t) Life (u) lotus
(v) flower (w) Buddah

2. Teacher check

Additional activities

- Research to produce an illustrated chart, poster or booklet detailing some aspects of Hinduism or Sikhism.

- Design a colour key to be used on an outline map of Asia to show the dominant religions in each country.

Islam in India – 1

Although the majority of India's people follow Hinduism, after Hinduism, Islam is the most practised religion in India.

Islam was brought to some coastal areas of India by traders in the 7th century CE but it was the Muslim invasions of the 11th and 12th centuries that introduced the religion to the rest of the subcontinent.

Muslims live their lives based on what is known as the Five Pillars of Islam. The five pillars are: faith, prayer, charity to others, fasting and pilgrimage.

Faith: Muslims believe that Allah is the one and only God. The last prophet to communicate with Allah was Mohammed, to whom he gave the Koran, the holy book of Islam. By following the word of the Koran, all Muslims worship Allah.

Prayer: Five times a day, Muslims are called to prayer by the muezzin at a mosque. He stands on a minaret facing in the direction of Mecca, the holy city of Islam. A mosque is an Islamic temple. A minaret is a tall tower with an onion-shaped crown and is part of a mosque. Before entering a mosque, a person must remove his or her shoes and the face, hands and feet are washed.

Charity to others: Muslims believe that everything belongs to Allah. Any personal possessions are only on loan from him so people should always be willing to give freely to anyone in need. At the end of Ramadan, Muslims give gifts of food to the needy so that they too can celebrate the end of the month of fasting.

Fasting: Ramadan is the ninth month of the Islamic calendar. During Ramadan, all healthy Muslims from about the age of 12, fast between sunrise and sunset. They reflect on their lives and the will of Allah. It is like a spiritual spring cleaning. They visit the mosque more often and read from the Koran. After sunset each day, they have a meal with family and friends.

The first three days of Shawwal, the tenth month, is a very special time for all Muslims. It is the festival of Eid ul-Fitr, which means 'the feast of breaking the fast'. As well as praying to Allah, people decorate their homes, give gifts to each other and enjoy special meals together. In Islamic countries, these three days are public holidays.

Pilgrimage: Mecca, in Saudi Arabia, is the holiest meeting place of the Islamic religion. It is the birthplace of the last prophet, Mohammed. All Muslims are expected to make a pilgrimage to Mecca, at least once in their lives, if they can afford to. The annual pilgrimage to Mecca, known as the Hajj, takes place in the last month of the Islamic calendar. The Great Mosque in Mecca is the biggest mosque in the world. In its centre is the Kaaba, a huge, square building made of stone. Pilgrims kneel in concentric circles around the Kaaba so that they are all facing it. All over the world, mosques are designed so that when people pray, the faithful are facing the Kaaba.

The Hajj is also followed by a three-day celebration, the festival of Eid al-Adha which means 'the feast of sacrifice'. Muslims celebrate with worship to Allah and by exchanging gifts. This holiday commemorates the faith and obedience of the prophet Abraham, who was prepared to sacrifice his son, Ishmael, to Allah.

Islam in India – 2

To complete the puzzle, find the answers to the clues in the text on page 63.

Across

3. Islamic temple
4. Feast of sacrifice
6. Religious belief
8. Follower of Islam
10. Feast of breaking the fast
11. Tenth month of Islamic calendar
12. Act of worship
14. He calls the faithful to prayer
17. Annual pilgrimage
18. Obedient prophet
20. Going without food

Down

1. Shrine at Mecca
2. Act of giving
3. Last prophet
5. Son of Abraham
7. Holy journey
9. Towering spire
13. Month of fasting
14. Holiest place of Islam
15. Muslim religion
16. Sacred book of Islam
19. The one Islamic God

Buddhism

Buddhism was founded by Siddhattha Gautama in northern India in the 5th century BCE. He discovered how to achieve peace, free from the sufferings of life. He shared this wisdom with others so that they too could achieve this same perfect state.

1. **Research to find information to complete the cloze passage about Buddhism.**

   Buddhists believe in (a) r___________, which is the cycle of birth, death and rebirth. This cycle continues until a person gains (b) e___________ by following the teachings of Buddha and by (c) m___________. When the cycle is broken, a person is said to have reached the state of perfect peace which is known as (d) n___________. A collection of three books make up the sacred text of Buddhism and is known as the (e) T___________. The three books are known as the three (f) B___________ of (g) W___________.

   At the heart of Buddhism are three main beliefs:

   - Belief in Buddha
   - Belief in (h) D___________, the teachings of Buddha
   - Belief in (i) S___________, the Buddhist community.

   Buddha's teaching is divided into three parts, which are:

   - the (j) T___________ (k) S___________ of (l) B___________
   - the (m) F___________ (n) N___________ (o) T___________
   - and the (p) N___________ (q) E___________ (r) P___________.

   Symbols of Buddhism are:

   the (s) W___________ of (t) L___________.

   the (u) l___________ (v) f___________.

   images of (w) B___________.

2. **Use your research and information from the text to design a chart, poster or booklet giving more detailed information on an aspect of Buddhism.**

The story of Shibi Rana ....page 67

Objective

Creates an illustrated copy of a story from the *Mahabharata*.

Teacher information

- The *Mahabharata* (3rd century BCE) and *Ramayana* (1st century CE) are the national epics of India. The *Mahabharata* is primarily the story of Lord Krishna, and the *Ramayana*, the story of Lord Rama and Sita.

- The *Mahabharata* is a sacred Sanskrit poem that encompasses the essence of Indian culture. 'Mahabharata' means the 'great story of the Bharatas'. Bharata was an early ancestor of the Pandavas and Kauravas, the two arms of the family who fought against each other in the great war that is described in the epic poem.

- The earlier descendant kings of Bharata prospered in material wealth and also in strength of character. They lived and ruled according to the law of Dharma, which is righteousness. For them, a life without goodness was worthless. For the sake of this belief, they were even prepared to sacrifice their own lives. This is illustrated in the story of Shibi Rana.

- The *Mahabharata* is extremely important to the Hindu culture of South Asia and is considered a major text of Hinduism, explaining the human goals of duty, purpose, pleasure and freedom, and the complexity of human relationships.

- It is said that the *Mahabharata* is all-inclusive. What is contained in the *Mahabharata* may be found elsewhere but there is nothing that can be found elsewhere that is not contained in the *Mahabharata*. It is said to have been compiled by Vyasa (who according to Hindu tradition is in existence today) and the text was scribed by Garnesh, god of writing and wisdom and son of Lord Shiva.

Answers

Teacher check

Additional activities

- Write and perform a simple script based on this story from the *Mahabharata* to present to younger pupils.
- Design a poster listing the lessons learned from this story from the *Mahabharata*.

The story of Shibi Rana

This story comes from an ancient Indian poem, **The Mahabharata.** *It illustrates the belief that sacrifice is preferable to a life without goodness.*

King Shibi ruled in the kingdom of the mighty Kurus in the north of India. He was loved for his honesty and fairness to his subjects. One day, Dharmaraj, the king of all that is good, decided to put Shibi Rana to the test.

One day a dove flew to where Shibi Rana was relaxing in the palace garden.

'Oh, great king! Please give me shelter! I am being chased by an eagle that wants to eat me!'

The king knew he must give a safe haven to those in need and so he agreed to help the small bird.

Moments later, the eagle landed beside the king.

'Oh, great king! Please return my prey so that I do not die of hunger.'

With this request, the king was placed in an uncomfortable situation. What should he do? The eagle had a right to his food but in giving up the dove, he would be guilty of not protecting the weak from the strong. He spoke of this to the eagle.

After some discussion with the King, the eagle suggested, 'I shall give the dove his freedom but there are two conditions which must be upheld'. 'Firstly, you must give me a part of your flesh that is of equal weight as that of the doves. Secondly, you must not shed a single tear of pain as your flesh is being cut or I will not be able to eat it and you will have to give me the bird!'

To protect the defenceless dove, the king willingly agreed to this painful solution and a set of balance scales and a sharp knife were brought to him. The dove was placed in one tray of the scales and flesh from the king's right leg was placed in the other. But no matter how much flesh was taken, the scales did not balance and soon all the flesh from the King's right leg was gone. As the left leg was prepared for cutting, the eagle spotted tears in the king's eyes.

'Oh, great king!' cried the eagle; 'You are crying! I cannot eat your flesh. Give me the dove and I shall return your flesh and heal your wounds.'

But Shibi Rana replied, 'Oh no, great eagle! These are not tears of pain but tears of joy, for now my left leg may also be offered to protect the dove. If only one leg had been used, the other would have been denied the opportunity of sacrifice!'

At this, King Shibi's leg was miraculously restored and the eagle and the dove disappeared. In their places appeared Dharmaraj and Indra, the god of righteousness and the king of heaven. Shibi Rana had shown that he was prepared to sacrifice himself for his duty. For this, he was rewarded by the gods.

Fold sheets of plain A4 paper in half and use them to make an illustrated book of the story, depicting one scene on each page.

The *Ramayana* .... page 69

Objective

Creates an illustrated copy of the story of the *Ramayana*.

Teacher information

- The *Mahabharata* (3rd century BCE) and *Ramayana* (1st century CE) are the national epics of India. The *Mahabharata* is primarily the story of Lord Krishna, and the *Ramayana*, the story of Lord Rama and Sita.

- The *Ramayana* contains the teachings of ancient Hindu traditions which are as important to Hindus today as they have always been.

- The aim of the *Ramayana* is to give the common people, through narrative, the teachings of Hinduism.

- In Hinduism, there is one all-powerful god, Brahman, who has three forms, Brahma, Vishnu and Shiva.

- Rama is the seventh incarnation of Vishnu, the protector of the world. He is one of the lords who, according to Hindi tradition, rule the world. The other lords are Brahma (the creator) and Shiva (the destroyer). It is said that Rama was born on the banks of the ancient Sarayu River and this is where he goes, on his retirement, to return to his supreme existence as Lord Vishnu.

- Determine the lessons that are being taught in the story by examining the events involving different characters and how the outcome of these events affect the relationships or how the relationships determine the outcome of events.

- The events/relationships are among:
  – Rama and his brothers (generally)
  – the emperor of Ayodhya and his wife, Kaikeyi
  – the emperor and Rama
  – Kaikeyi and Rama
  – Kaikeyi and Bharata
  – Rama and Lakshmana
  – Rama and Bharata
  – Rama and Hanuman
  – Lakshmana and Bharata.

- The *Mahabharata* is the other great epic of ancient India. It is a poem that describes the development of Hindu moral law. At almost two million words in one hundred thousand verses, it is the longest poem in the world. The *Mahabharata* is extremely important to the Hindu culture of South Asia and is considered a major text of Hinduism. It aims to explain the human goals of duty, purpose, pleasure and freedom, and the relationships an individual has with society and the world as a whole.

Answers

Teacher check

Additional activities

- Write and perform a simple script based on this version of the *Ramayana* to present to younger pupils.

- Design a poster listing the lessons learned from this version of the *Ramayana*.

The Ramayana

According to Hindu beliefs, Rama is an incarnation of Lord Vishnu, one of the three incarnations of the all-powerful god, Brahman, who rule the world. The **Ramayana**, meaning 'the journey of Rama', tells the story of Rama who is sent into exile by his father, the emperor of Ayodhya.

The emperor has four sons—Rama, the eldest and heir to the kingdom, Bharata and the twins, Lakshmana and Shatrughna. The brothers have great love and respect for each other. There is no petty jealousy or rivalry among them.

Kaikeyi, the emperor's wife, wants Bharata to be heir to the throne, so she tricks her husband into sending Rama and Sita (his wife), into exile in the forest for 14 years. One of the twins, Lakshmana, goes with them as he cannot bear to be parted from his dear brother.

When the emperor dies and Bharata realises that he is to be the new ruler, he is outraged and goes to find Rama. But Rama refuses to return home to Ayodhya until his term of exile is finished.

Reluctantly, Bharata agrees to rule the kingdom but vows that if Rama does not return as soon as his time in exile is served, he will sacrifice his own life. Bharata never sits on the throne, nor wears the royal robes. Instead, he leaves Rama's sandals at the foot of the royal throne, awaiting the return of the rightful king.

Bharata rules well and the kingdom enjoys peace and prosperity but Bharata never forgives his mother for what she has done.

Not long before Rama is due to return, his wife, Sita, is kidnapped by Ravana, the demon king. Rama, Lakshmana and Hanuman, the monkey warrior, follow Ravana to Lanka, his island kingdom. Here the demon king is defeated and Sita is released.

Rama gratefully tells Hanuman that he has the same love and respect for him as he does for his three brothers. Rama asks Hanuman to hurry to Ayodhya as he is fearful that Bharata may carry out his promise.

As Rama, Sita and Lakshmana arrive in Ayodhya on the night of the new moon, their way is lit by thousands of small lamps. Bharata leads the procession to greet them and there follows a great celebration.

Rama is crowned emperor and intends to make Lakshmana his main advisor. Lakshmana insists that this honour should go to Bharata who has shown great loyalty to Rama and ruled the kingdom successfully for 14 years.

The festival of Diwali, which means 'rows of lighted lamps', is celebrated in India each year to remember Rama's joyous return from exile.

Fold sheets of plain A4 paper in half and use them to make an illustrated book of the *Ramayana*, depicting one scene on each page.

Landmarks

The Taj Mahal .... page 71

Objective

Uses information in a text to present an illustrated version of the given text on the Taj Mahal.

Teacher information

- Regarded as one of the new seven wonders of the world, it is said that the architectural beauty of the Taj Mahal has never been equalled. It is a magnificent monument of Mughal architecture. The Mughals were the Muslim rulers of India from the early 16th century to the mid-19th century. The Taj Mahal's majestic beauty is enhanced at dawn and sunset when the sun's low rays bathe it in a golden light causing its white marble to sparkle like a jewel. Even at night, basking in the moonlight, the Taj Mahal exudes grace and beauty. It is said that Shah Jahan decreed that it should be build at a place where nothing would cast a shadow upon it.

- The Taj Mahal was made a UNESCO World Heritage Site in 1983.

Additional activities

- With additional information from the internet, draw an accurate plan of the Taj Mahal complex.

- Research to discover the fate of Shah Jahan. Present the story as a comic strip.

India's red forts .... page 72

Objective

Completes a tourist guide for the red forts of Agra and Delhi using the given text.

Teacher information

- Agra was just a small town before the Mughals decided to make it the capital of their Empire. It was during the reign of Akbar, the third Mughal emperor, that the main part of the Red Fort of Agra was built. Most of the elaborate buildings inside the fort were constructed under the orders of Shah Jahan.

- The Red Fort of Agra lies on the banks of the Yamuna River, a short distance from the Taj Mahal. It was made a UNESCO World Heritage Site in 1983.

- The Red Fort in Delhi was the seat of Mughal political and economic power. Internal and foreign affairs were administered from there. The construction of Shahjahanabad and the fort within it was completed within ten years. It was the only Mughal city of its size to be designed and built as a living, thriving community. Such was the strength of this community that even when the Mughal Empire declined, it has continued to thrive to the present day.

- The Red Fort in Delhi was made a UNESCO World Heritage Site in 2007.

Additional activities

- With additional information from the internet, draw an plan of either fort.

- Research to discover the history of the Peacock Throne and the Koh-i-noor diamond.

The Lotus Temple .... page 73

Objective

Constructs an explosion chart using the given text on the Lotus Temple to find out more the Baha'i religion and its houses of worship.

Teacher information

- There are only seven Baha'i houses of worship worldwide, with the construction of others underway. The first was built in the early 20th century in Turkmenistan. It was finally demolished in 1963 after having been badly damaged during an earthquake many years before.

Additional activities

- Choose one aspect of your explosion chart to study in detail. Use a graphic organiser to arrange your notes. Using these notes, give an oral presentation to the class.

- Draw a plan of the Lotus Temple, including the pools and gardens.

The Taj Mahal

Just to the south of the walled city of Agra in northern India, along a bend in the Yamuna River, lies the magnificent Taj Mahal, the 'jewel of Muslim art in India'. For more than 350 years, this stunning example of Mughal architecture has graced the landscape and been the ultimate goal for millions of travellers from within India and abroad.

Built with jewel-encrusted white marble, the Taj Mahal is a memorial to the wife of Shah Jahan, a Mughal emperor. Mumtaz Mahal died after giving birth to their fourteenth child. Stricken with grief, the emperor forbade celebration in the royal court for two years and in 1632, a year after her death, he gave the order for the memorial to be built.

Materials for the grand mausoleum were gathered from within the subcontinent and beyond. The white marble from Rajasthan was inlaid with many kinds of precious and semiprecious stones from as far away as China, Sri Lanka and Arabia. With supposedly twenty thousand labourers and one thousand elephants employed on the project, it was finally completed in 1653.

The rare beauty of the Taj Mahal is embodied in the blend of traditional Mughal and Hindu decorative features and the simplicity of its symmetrical design. In the whole complex, there is only one deviation from this symmetry. In the burial chamber lie the tombs of Shah Jahan and his beloved wife. Her tomb is placed in the centre of the chamber while his, which is larger, lies to the west of hers.

The Taj Mahal generally refers to the white marble mausoleum but it is not an isolated building. The Taj Mahal complex includes the huge gateway entrance to the complex and two red sandstone buildings standing one on either side of the Taj. The one on the western side, facing Mecca, is a mosque. The other is there solely for the purpose of symmetry. The complex is enclosed on three sides by decorated red walls. The fourth side is open to the river.

The Persian-style gardens of the Taj Mahal are also laid out in symmetrical design. The four main sections are further divided by walkways lined with trees and fountains. The trees, planted alternately, are cypress (representing death) and fruit trees (representing life). The raised marble water tank reflects the image of the mausoleum. It is this view of the Taj Mahal that is familiar to millions of people across the globe.

In 1983, the Taj Mahal was listed as a UNESCO World Heritage Site. The Indian government is obliged to maintain this historical gem for future generations. Pollution from industry and automobile emissions is currently the greatest threat, and is damaging its white marble surface.

On plain paper, present an illustrated version of this information as a booklet.

Suggestions for illustrations to include in the booklet:

- a map of Asia to show location of places mentioned and where building materials came from
- a cartoon strip of the story behind the building of the Taj Mahal
- a plan of the Taj Mahal complex
- a time line marked at 50 year intervals from 1600 to 2050. Insert dates from the text plus the year of your birth and the year of today.

India's red forts

India is awash with magnificent landmarks—examples of architectural extravagance that offer glimpses into the country's fascinating and ancient history.

Two such places are the Red Fort of Agra (Agra Fort) and the Red Fort in Delhi (Lal Quila).

The first of India's red forts was built in Agra during the reign of the Mughal emperor, Akbar the Great. At this time, Agra was the capital of the Mughal Empire. Constructed from red sandstone, the Red Fort was initially designed as a military garrison but was later developed to include many lavish buildings.

During his reign as emperor, Akbar's grandson, Shah Jahan, moved the Mughal capital from Agra to a location to the north of Delhi which he named Shahjahanabad. This new, walled city was designed by Shah Jahan and he was heavily involved in its construction. Inside the city were many markets, gardens, mosques and fine houses and the red sandstone fortress, Lal Quila, which is double the size of the fort of Agra.

The table includes just some of the buildings within each fort.

Red Fort of Agra	Red Fort in Delhi
Jahangiri Mahal: main palace for women of the royal household	*Chatta Chowk:* covered markets selling silks and jewels to the wealthy
Khas Mahal: palace built for Shah Jahan's two favourite daughters; overlooks Angoori Bagh (Grape Garden)	*Naubat Khana:* bandstand for musicians and other public entertainment
Shish Mahal: bathing palace decorated with many mirrors	*Mumtaz Mahal:* palace for the women of the royal court
Musamman Burj: octagonal tower; home of an emperor's chief wife; has view of Taj Mahal	*Rang Mahal:* 'Palace of Colours', home of an emperor's chief wife
Diwan-i-khas: hall where a private meeting with the emperor was allowed	*Royal baths:* spacious Turkish baths with a decorative fountain
Diwan-i-am: hall where a public meeting with the emperor was allowed; location of elaborate Peacock Throne	*Shahi Burj:* octagonal tower used as Shah Jahan's personal study
Moti Masjid: the 'Pearl Mosque', constructed with white marble	*Jama Masjid:* largest and most well-known mosque in India
Machchhi Bhawan: built exclusively to rear goldfish for Shah Jahan's amusement	*Lahore Gate:* main entrance into the fort; the Indian prime minister delivers the Independence Day address on 15 August each year from here

Use the information in the text to create a tourist guide for the red forts of Agra and Delhi. Illustrate your guide with sketches of pictures from the internet.

The Lotus Temple

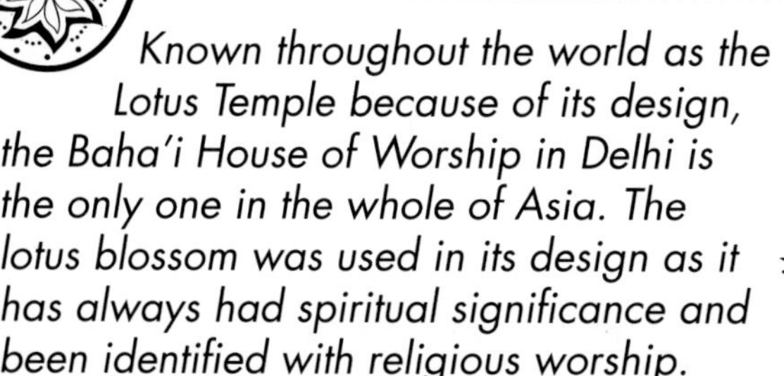

Known throughout the world as the Lotus Temple because of its design, the Baha'i House of Worship in Delhi is the only one in the whole of Asia. The lotus blossom was used in its design as it has always had spiritual significance and been identified with religious worship.

In the Mahabharata, an ancient poem of great importance in the Hindu tradition, Lord Brahma (the creator god) grew from the lotus flower which was growing out of the navel of the protector god, Lord Vishnu. Avalokitesvara, one of the most popular Buddhist beings, is always pictured holding a lotus blossom.

The Lotus Temple is a place of worship for the Baha'i faith, one of the youngest of the world's religions, founded in the 19th century by Bahaullah. According to followers of this faith, Bahaullah is a messenger of God, just as Jesus Christ is in the Christian religion and Mohammed in Islam.

Like every other Baha'i house of worship, the Lotus Temple is open to anyone for religious worship. Baha'i Law states that a house of worship is for people of any faith to come and praise God. The key message of the Baha'i faith is that the whole of humanity is one single race and the time has come to break down the walls of separation and prejudice and unite all people as one global community.

Within the temple, while holy scriptures from any religion may be read and its prayers sung, musical instruments may not be played. Also, sermons may not be preached and ritualistic ceremonies may not be practised.

While all Baha'i houses of worship are unique from each other, they do share certain architectural features, some of which are specified by Baha'i scripture. In response to the law stating that each house of worship must have a nine-sided circular shape, the Lotus Temple has 27 marble 'petals', arranged in sets of three to give its nine sides.

No images, pictures or statues may be displayed in a house of worship and no pulpits or altars may be included in the design. Portable lecterns may be used to hold a book of scriptures for readers. All present houses of worship have domes but this is not required by Baha'i law.

The nine doors of the Lotus Temple open into the central hall which can hold 2500 people, and out on to reflecting pools, representing the green leaves of the lotus flower.

The design of the Lotus Temple created many problems for the 800 people who toiled for over five years to build it, but their efforts have been well rewarded. It has received numerous awards for architectural excellence and many accolades have been bestowed upon it.

Evening is the best time to view this magnificent edifice as the marble shines like a diamond in the rays of the setting sun.

Use the information on this page as a catalyst to construct an explosion chart for finding out more about the Lotus Temple and the Baha'i religion.

Suggestions for explosion chart:

- details about the construction of Lotus Temple: architect, design, dates, materials, workforce, problems, awards
- information about the Baha'i religion: founder, scriptures, laws, festivals, other houses of worship
- details about the lotus flower: scientific name, species, life cycle, growing conditions, spiritual significance

Landmarks

Objective

Uses a text to write a newspaper report about the discovery of the Ajanta Caves, including how the discovery might affect different groups of people.

Teacher information

- The cave temples of Ajanta, which are exclusively Buddhist, were excavated from a horseshoe-shaped ravine along the Waghora River. The 29 caves are numbered according to their position along the cliff face. This numbering system does not correspond to the order in which the caves were excavated. The caves include temples of the Theravada and Mahayana forms of Buddhism. The stunning Mahayana murals in caves 1, 2, 16, and 17 are major highlights of a visit to the caves. These murals, dating from the 5th century, are well preserved and they are one of the India's many great cultural treasures.

- The Ellora Caves are numbered from south to north, corresponding to the order in which they were excavated, with the exception of Cave 21. Caves 1 to 12, to the south, are Buddhist temples circa 7th and 8th centuries CE. Caves 13 to 29 are Hindu temples and include some temples which had previously been Buddhist temples, circa 7th to the 9th centuries CE. The five upper caves are Jain temples circa 9th century CE.

- The Elephanta caves were excavated to create columns within the large caverns in which sculptures and frescos were created. The huge temple complex houses a main chamber with two smaller side chambers and many courtyards and shrines.

Answers

Teacher check

Additional activities

- From the text, write as many quiz questions as possible. Collate and refine all questions, then hold a class quiz.

- Choose one of the caves to research further. Present a brochure including a plan of the caves and illustrations of the more famous carvings or frescos.

Temple caves

Scattered across India are a number of temple caves, some dating back over two thousand years. They are not natural caves but have been hewn from solid rock. The walls and ceilings are decorated with vibrant frescos and magnificent sculptures, crafted by hand using basic tools like a hammer and chisel. In the state of Maharashtra, on the western side of the country, are three of India's most famous temple caves.

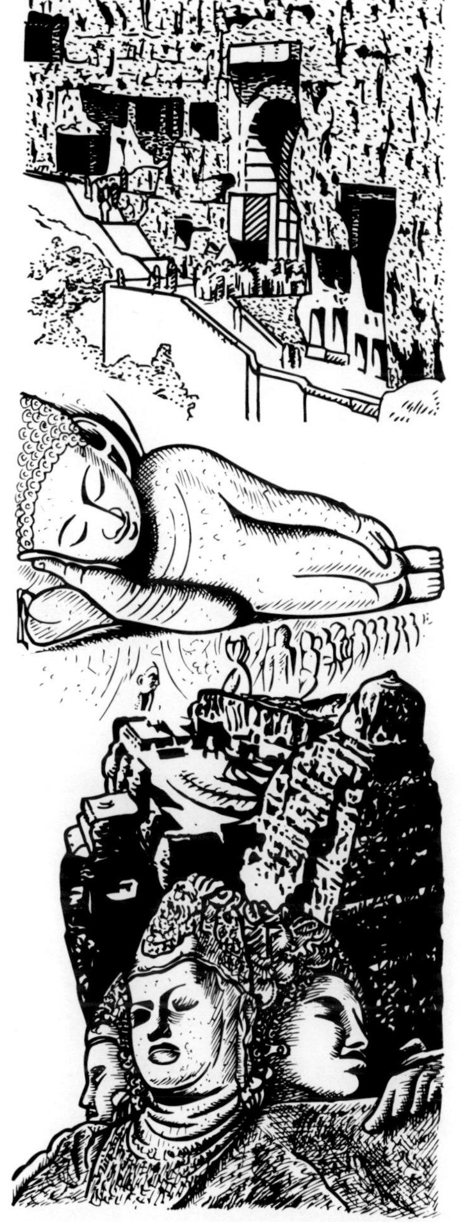

*The Buddhist caves at **Ajanta** are located in a cliff, overlooking a beautiful river valley. The 29 caves, dating from the 2nd century BCE to the 6th century CE, include monasteries and temples. Cave number 26, a hall for prayer and meditation, contains the superb carved statue of the reclining Buddha.*

The frescos of the Ajanta temples are of particular interest to visitors. They illustrate many Buddhist legends with a vibrancy characteristic of Indian art.

It was not until 1819 that the caves at Ajanta, which had fallen into abandonment, were discovered. A British army officer came across the caves by accident one day while he was on a hunting expedition.

*The 34 **Ellora** caves, which include Hindu, Jain and Buddhist temples, are famous for their amazing architecture. The most magnificent example is the Hindu Kailasa Temple. It was designed as a representation of Mount Kailasa in the Himalayas, home to Lord Shiva. The temple is a massive, spectacular tribute to the 7000 workers who toiled for over 150 years to complete it.*

Because Ellora stands on an ancient trade route, the caves were never lost nor abandoned but were visited regularly by travellers to the area.

*Located 10 kilometres to the west of Mumbai, in the Arabian Sea, is a small island which is the site of the **Elephanta** caves. The temples date back to the 6th century CE and are dedicated to Lord Shiva.*

The colossal carving of Trimurti Sadasiva is an imposing image of Shiva. At seven metres high, the sculpture shows three of Shiva's five faces. The right half-face depicts Shiva as a young person, resembling Brahma, the creator. The left half-face depicts him as an older person, resembling Shiva, the destroyer. In the central full-face, Shiva is meditating and at peace—resembling Vishnu, the preserver.

All three sites are on the UNESCO World Heritage List. The Ajanta and Ellora caves were inscribed in 1983, and the Elephanta caves in 1987. UNESCO seeks to preserve examples of cultural and natural heritage across the globe so that they are available for future generations to enjoy for education, leisure or spiritual fulfilment.

Write a newspaper report about the discovery of the caves at Ajanta.

Include an eye-catching title and excerpts from conversations with the British officer, an archaeologist, a historian, local residents and local businesses, all explaining how the discovery will affect them.

Folktales and legends

The Ganga legend

Objective

Reads and comprehends a narrative about the legend of the Ganges River.

Teacher information

- The Ganges begins at a place called Goumukh, which is a glacier. Its name, 'Goumukh', means 'cow mouth'. Seven different streams and rivers combine to form the Ganges. On its way to the ocean, the Ganges flows by approximately 30 cities, 70 towns and thousands of villages. More than 450 million people are directly or indirectly dependent on the river and its basin.

- Although the Ganges is considered to be the most revered river in the world, it is also one of the dirtiest in terms of pollution. It is estimated that 1 billion litres of mostly untreated raw sewage goes directly into the river daily. This includes household rubbish, food, human and animal remains, and organic waste. Besides the sacred Hindu practice of placing cremated human remains in the holy river, the carcasses of cattle, which are sacred to them, are also placed in the river.

Answers

Answers may vary:

1. The goddess, Ganga, is the daughter of the mountain god, Himalaya, where the Ganges has its source. The Hindi people believe the Ganges is the earthly form of this goddess.

2. He wanted to carry it out to prove his supremacy. It involved allowing a horse to roam the Earth and for it to return unchallenged to his kingdom.

3. As Lord Indra feared King Sagar's power, he kidnapped the horse and hid it at the dwelling of Kapil Muni.

4. He killed them because he was interrupted from a deep meditation by the noise they were making and found them attacking his house.

5. (d), (a), (c), (b)

6. Because Lord Shiva let the Ganga flow through his hair to break its fall to Earth and it parted into seven smaller streams instead of one torrent.

7. It was formed when the river neared the ocean and followed its own course and divided into one hundred mouths.

8. Answers should include bathing in it to wash away sins; cremating bodies at the river's edge and throwing in the ashes; bringing the bones of dead loved ones to place in the river.

Additional activity

- Type in the keywords 'bathing in Ganges River' into a search engine to view families and groups of people bathing in the sacred river. (There are many pilgrimage sites along the river.)

Two Indian folktales

Objective

Reads, comprehends and compares two Indian folktales.

Teacher information

- These two folktales are from the *Panchatantra*, a legendary collection of short stories from India. They were originally written in the 2nd century BCE to help instruct the young sons of the reigning king with the correct values and governing skills needed in life. Each *Panchatantra* tale is accompanied by a moral. A 'brahmin' can be described as a lay preacher or educator, someone who had a high place in the Hindu faith.

Answers

2. (a) Teacher check
   (b) Answers should indicate:
       Folktale 1: Don't act in haste or jump to quick conclusions.
       Folktale 2: Pay attention to what needs to be done;
                   be realistic about building castles in the air.

   (c) – (e) Teacher check

Additional activity

- Read and retell other Panchatantra tales orally or as a narrative. A useful website is:
  <http://www.culturalindia.net/indian-folktales/panchatantra-tales/>

The Ganga legend – 1

The Ganges River flows more than 2500 kilometres from its source in a glacial ice cave high in the Himalayas in northern India, to the Bay of Bengal in the Indian Ocean in the west. It is named after a goddess, Ganga, the daughter of the mountain god, Himalaya. The Hindi people believe the Ganges is the earthly form of this goddess. They worship the Ganges and regard it as a sacred river. There are many stories concerning the origin of the Ganges. The following version is based on one of the most popular.

King Sagar, ruler of Ayodhya, had sixty thousand sons. The king was a powerful and fearless man and had defeated all the demons on Earth. One day, the king decided to perform an ancient horse ceremony called the 'Ashwamedha sacrifice' to show his supremacy. This involved setting a horse free to roam at will over the land and for it to return to him without being captured or attacked.

However, Lord Indra, the king of the gods, feared King Sagar's power and plotted against him. He kidnapped the horse and hid it outside the secluded dwelling of a wise old sage, Kapil Muni.

The sixty thousand sons searched the mountains, the rivers, the plains and the oceans for the horse. At last they came upon the sage's abode. Mistaking the sage as the kidnapper, they began to attack the house. Kapil Muni, deep in meditation, was interrupted by the disturbance. He opened his eyes in anger and used his fiery gaze to burn the sixty thousand princes and reduce them to ashes.

For many years, the sons' souls wandered as ghosts as their last rites had not been administered. Finally, one of King Sagar's grandchildren went in search of Kapil Muni to ask how their souls might be released. The sage advised him that the waters of the goddess Ganga, who resided in heaven, could cleanse their remains and they would be set free.

King Sagar prayed and pleaded to Ganga for several years. His grandson, then his great-grandson, then his great-great grandson tried ... It was his seventh generation descendent, Bhagiratha, who finally persuaded Ganga to descend to Earth.

As the Ganga rushed towards Earth, Bhagiratha prayed to Lord Shiva to help lessen the severity of the falling waters and prevent a catastrophe. Lord Shiva held out his long, matted hair and let the waters flow gently through it and land on the Himalayas in seven streams. These streams flowed into one to become the Ganges. Bhagiratha led the river down to the sea, where it followed its own course and divided into one hundred mouths to form the mighty Ganges Delta. One of the streams reached the place where the ashes of the sixty thousand sons lay and freed their souls.

To this day, bathing in the Ganga is believed to wash away sins. People also bring the bones of their dead loved ones to place in the river or cremate their bodies at the river's edge and throw in the ashes. These actions are believed to lead to the salvation of the deceased.

The Ganga legend – 2

Answer the questions.

1. Briefly explain the connection between the goddess, Ganga, and the Ganges River.

2. Why did King Sagar want to carry out an Ashwamedha Sacrifice and what did this involve?

3. What part did Lord Indra play in the Ashwamedha Sacrifice?

4. Why did Kapil Muni kill the sixty thousand sons?

5. Order these events from 1 to 4.

    ☐ (a) King Sagar prayed to the goddess.

    ☐ (b) Bhagiratha asked for Shiva's assistance.

    ☐ (c) The Ganga began to descend to Earth.

    ☐ (d) The sage suggested how the son's souls could be freed.

6. Why did the Ganga form seven streams upon landing on Earth?

7. How was the Ganges Delta formed?

8. Describe some of the practices connected with the Ganges.

Two Indian folktales

1. Read the two folktales from India.

Folktale 1: The mongoose and the brahmin's wife

Long ago, a faithful brahmin and his devoted wife were eagerly expecting their first child. In due course, they were overjoyed to have a healthy son. The brahmin's wife wanted to have a pet who would not only be a companion to their child, but also protect it. After much debate, they chose a mongoose.

One day, they decided to leave their child in the mongoose's charge while they went out. Shortly after they left, a dangerous cobra slithered into their home. The mongoose viciously attacked the cobra and succeeded in killing it.

The couple arrived home to find the mongoose's mouth stained with blood. The farmer's wife jumped to the conclusion that the mongoose had killed her child. Without thinking, she threw a heavy chair at the mongoose and killed it.

Her gaze then drifted to the back of the room. The cobra lay dead near her sleeping child's cradle. The farmer's wife turned to her husband in anguish ...

Folktale 2: The brahmin's dream

An impoverished brahmin once lived in a small village. He was so poor that he had to beg for food. This he kept in an earthen pot hung up beside his bed.

One lucky day, the brahmin obtained enough rice gruel for several meals. He was so pleased, he went to sleep with a smile on his face. He dreamt that the pot began to overflow with gruel which meant he could earn many silver coins selling it if famine came to the land. With the coins he could buy a pair of goats. The goats would eventually produce a herd which he could trade for cows and bulls. The milk and butter and curd products from the cows could be sold. Then he could buy a house and marry and have children! His children would run merrily around the garden.

In his dream, the brahmin thought it best to scold the children for making too much noise. Still dreaming, he picked up a stick near his bed and began to swirl it in the air to get the children's attention. The stick hit the pot of gruel, which broke and splattered its contents all over the floor. The brahmin woke to find his dreams were shattered ...

2. On a separate sheet of paper, complete the following activities.

(a) Identify the orientation (who, when, where, what), complication (to the main character) and events in chronological order for each folktale.

(b) Explain the moral of each folktale.

(c) Write another suitable title for each folktale.

(d) Add another short paragraph to each folktale that shows what the main character would have learned from the experience.

(e) Explain two similarities and two differences between each folktale.

Folktales and legends

Garnesh and Krishna pages 81–82

Objective

Reads and comprehends legends about the births of two Indian gods, Garnesh and Krishna.

Teacher information

- Garnesh and Krishna are two of the best known and widely worshipped of the Indian divinities. In Hindu culture, Garnesh is known as the god of entrances, success and overcoming obstacles. He is also known as Garnesh, Ganesa or Ganapati. Garnesh is easily identified by his elephant head, four arms, one tusk (the other being broken off), pot belly and two legs (one resting on the ground and the other raised). Krishna is considered to be the god of love and happiness. He is depicted in many forms—as a baby, child and young man. His most common pose is with a flute surrounded by adoring gopis (daughters of cowherders). The mythical prophecy of Krishna slaying Kamsa occurs when Krishna was 12 years of age.

Answers

1. Yellow (Garnesh): an animal was involved, came back to life, father was Lord Shiva, mother was Parvathi, was beheaded

   Blue (Krishna): contained a prophecy, mother was Devaki, number eight was important, father was Vasudeva, involved exchange of babies

   Green (both): Hindu gods, violent events occurred, born to perform special tasks, concerned with births, legends from India

2. Teacher check

3. (c), (d), (a), (b)

4. Teacher check

Additional activity

- Read and retell other stories involving Garnesh or Krishna. A useful website is:
  <http://indianmythology.com/finish/storycategory.php?parent=7>

The anger-eating demon page 83

Objective

Reads and comprehends an ancient Buddhist story.

Teacher information

- Buddhist teachings called the demon described in the story as an 'anger-eating' demon. Becoming angry with someone can make that person even worse, just as the demon fed on the anger of others.

Answers

1. Answers should indicate it teaches us to not let anger overcome you. Problems can be solved through kindness and compassion towards the object of our anger.

2. huge, ugly, vulgar, disgusting, fearsome, brazen

3. (a) briskly   (b) slowly   (c) rudely   (d) angrily   (e) entirely
   (f) immediately

4. Teacher check

Additional activity

- Make a list of further adjectives and adverbs used in the story. (There are also some adjectival and adverbial phrases and clauses used to describe some nouns and verbs.)

Garnesh and Krishna – 1

Garnesh and Krishna are both Hindu gods. The legends of their births are popular tales in Indian mythology.

Legend 1: The birth of Garnesh

Long ago, Lord Shiva, god of death and destruction, was away at war, leaving his wife, Parvathi, alone at home. She became increasingly concerned that no-one was there to guard the entrance to her home. Parvathi came up with the idea of giving birth to a son who could perform this task for her. She used her powers as a goddess to create their son, Garnesh.

Parvathi instructed Garnesh to stand guard at the entrance to her home and under no circumstance was he to let anyone through without her consent. This he did willingly and conscientiously.

In due course, Lord Shiva arrived home. Garnesh, who had not yet met his father and was following his mother's instructions, refused to let him enter. Lord Shiva was so enraged that he drew his sword and cut off Garnesh's head.

Parvathi was infuriated when she discovered what had occurred. Lord Shiva, wanting to make amends for his mistake, agreed to bring Garnesh back to life. This he would do by taking the head of the first living animal he found. The first creature was an elephant. Lord Shiva took the head and recreated his son with the head of an elephant.

Legend 2: The birth of Krishna

King Kamsa, ruler of the kingdom of Mathura, was a wicked, evil man. He would do anything to promote his own power and glory. One day, he heard a heavenly voice from the sky announce, 'Kamsa! Your end is coming! The eighth child of your sister, Devaki, will be responsible for your death!'

Kamsa was so incensed, he imprisoned his sister and her husband, Vasudeva. He then went about killing every child of the couple as each was born. The first seven children were all boys. Just before midnight as Devaki's eighth child was being born, a god, Lord Vishnu, appeared. He told Vasudeva to carry this boy child across the Yamuna River to the town of Gokul. There he was to swap him with Yashoda's child, who had just had a girl.

Vasudeva placed the boy who was to become the god, Krishna, in a basket and set off. Miraculously, the prison doors opened for him and the waters of the Yamuna River parted for him to walk across. There he exchanged his son for Yashoda's daughter and returned. The baby's cries awakened Kamsa, who went to the prison chamber. Even when Devaki and Vasudeva informed him the child was a girl and could not hurt him, he still prepared to kill her.

However, the baby slipped out of his grasp and rose up in the air. In a sweet, lilting voice she exclaimed, 'I am the goddess, Devi, born as a baby to fool you. Your real enemy is alive and well. Devaki's and Vasudeva's child will come back to kill you and bring your wicked rule to an end.' With that, Devi disappeared.

Garnesh and Krishna – 2

Answer the questions.

1. Use the key to correctly highlight details below from the two legends.

Details associated with: *Garnesh – yellow*   *Krishna – blue*   *Both – green*

Hindu gods	contained a prophecy	mother was Devaki
an animal was involved	came back to life	number eight was important
father was Lord Shiva	violent events occurred	born to perform special tasks
concerned with births	mother was Parvathi	involved exchange of babies
was beheaded	father was Vasudeva	legends from India

2. Describe an event that occurred before these three events from the first legend.

- Parvathi became incensed when she realised what Lord Shiva had done.

- Garnesh followed his mother's wishes conscientiously.

- Lord Shiva searched for a live animal.

____

____

3. Order these events in the second legend from 1 to 4.

☐   (a)   The waters of the Yamuna River parted.

☐   (b)   A goddess reminded Kamsa about his future.

☐   (c)   Devaki and Vasudeva were sent to a prison chamber.

☐   (d)   Lord Vishnu advised Vasudeva.

4. Compose two short paragraphs to explain what might have occurred next in each legend.

Legend 1: ____

____

____

Legend 2: ____

____

____

The anger-eating demon

This story is based on an ancient Buddhist tale. An important religion in India, the Buddhist faith uses these kinds of stories to teach about how to lead a good life.

Long ago, there lived a wise and distinguished emperor. He had to leave his vast kingdom for a short time to visit other rulers. As the emperor trotted briskly off on his sturdy mount, his loyal followers went about their daily chores.

During the emperor's absence, a huge, ugly, vulgar demon arrived at the palace gates. He was so disgusting that the palace guards and advisors froze in horror. This enabled the fearsome demon to enter the palace grounds, amble slowly towards the royal audience hall and seat himself decisively on the emperor's throne. Seeing the brazen demon on the throne quickly jolted the guards and advisors back to reality.

'Get off that throne!' they shouted angrily. 'Who do you think you are?'

The demon rudely yelled back at them. To their surprise, he grew a few centimetres in height and girth. This angered them even more. They screamed at the demon again and told him his head would be cut off if he didn't depart immediately. Swords were flashed and more threats and insults made. The revolting demon simply grew even larger and became more grotesque.

It was at this point the emperor returned. He viewed the scene and immediately knew what to do. 'Welcome to my palace', he said warmly. 'Has anyone offered you something to eat or drink?'

The demon began to look a bit smaller and less repulsive. The guards and advisors realised what the emperor was doing and joined in making thoughtful and kind-hearted comments. Gradually the demon shrank in size and looked less offensive until one final friendly comment caused him to disappear entirely.

Answer the questions.

1. In your own words, explain what you think this story is trying to teach.

____

____

____

2. List the adjectives in the second paragraph used to describe the demon.

____

____

3. Write the adverb used to describe each of these verbs in the story.

(a) trotted __________   (b) amble __________   (c) yelled __________

(d) shouted __________   (e) disappear __________   (f) knew __________

4. On the back of this sheet, list more positive and negative comments that could have been said to make the demon reduce or enlarge in size.

The arts

Objective

Reads and comprehends information about Indian handicrafts.

Teacher information

- The first references to Indian handicrafts can be found from the Indus Valley Civilisation (3300–1700 BCE). At first handicrafts were made for day-to-day use until people began to desire beauty, and so designs and motifs started to develop. Historic Indian literature has revealed that Indian crafts were an integral part of religious rituals and ceremonies. This can be seen in the many stone sculptures of Buddha in India.

Answers

1. (a) parents/family   (b) religious
   (c) designs   (d) wood

2. 'Many rural communities are supported by the sale of these crafts.' (Paragraph 1)

3. Possible answers: To prevent the poaching of tigers for their hide. To protect tigers. To conserve tigers.

4. Teacher check

Additional activity

- Collect different coloured beads and fishing wire for pupils to use to craft necklaces and bracelets. Display their handicrafts.

Objective

Completes a cloze exercise about historical paintings and murals of India.

Teacher information

- There are 29 caves at Ajanta, Maharashtra. They are believed to have been used for shelter during the rainy monsoon months by travelling Buddhist monks. For over a thousand years, the caves lay hidden in the jungle until discovered by an Englishman, John Smith. The Ajanta caves have been classified as a UNESCO World Heritage Site since 1983.

Answers

1. murals	2. fat	3. animals
4. carved	5. ceilings	6. busy
7. century	8. chisel	9. hay
10. cow	11. outlines	12. glue
13. create	14. bacteria	15. tourists
16. lighting		

Additional activity

- Ask pupils to use an array of earthy-coloured chalks (such as browns, oranges, yellows, greens and blues) to sketch an important scene from their lives. The scene could show a birthday party, holiday, an exciting event, moving house etc. Pupils write a small synopsis of the event underneath the scene. Display all of the pupils' artwork together on a wall to create a mural.

Objective

Analyses a painting by an Indian artist depicting a scene of India.

Teacher information

- Pupils use the resource centre/Internet to choose a painting by an Indian artists to analyse. Some famous Indian artists include: MF Husain; Ram Kumar; Manjit Bawa; Krishan Khanna; Amrita Sher-Gil
- Types of paint mediums include oil painting, acrylics and watercolours.

Answers

Answers will vary.

Additional activity

- Choose one painting and enlarge it for the class to view. Complete an analysis of it as a class. Allow pupils to express their feelings about the painting. Ask the questions: 'Why do we not all feel the same way about it—not all 'like' or 'dislike' it?' Explain that art is 'subjective'.

The handicrafts of India

India produces the largest variety of handicrafts in the world. Craftsmen use traditional skills which have been handed down from one generation to the next. Many rural communities are supported by the sale of these crafts. Some handicrafts include embroidery, jewellery, toys, puppets, textiles, and items made from clay, ivory, glass, leather, metal, wood, papier-mâché and stone.

Many Indian handicrafts exhibit intricate designs and patterns and most vary from one region to the next. Some designs include spiral or curvy lines, vines, arches and domes, deities, crescent moons and stars. A great number are made for religious rites and rituals. Expensive materials such as ivory, gems and marble are used to create beautiful handicrafts.

Leatherwork is crafted from camel, deer, and, previously, tiger hide. Metals used for handicrafts include brass, copper, iron, bell metal, gold, silver and zinc. Woodwork materials include walnut and deodar (a type of cedar), sandalwood, teakwood and jackfruit tree. Stonework utilises sandstone, greenstone, marble and semiprecious stones (agate, amethyst, topaz etc.).

1. **Complete the sentences.**

    (a) Indian people usually learn their handicraft skills from their ___________________.

    (b) A large number of handicrafts are made for ___________________ purposes.

    (c) Vines, moons, stars and domes are types of ___________________ on Indian handicrafts.

    (d) Handicrafts are carved from different types of stone and ___________________.

2. **Underline the sentence in the text which explains that people living in country areas in India often rely on the sale of their handicrafts for their livelihoods.**

3. **Why do you think leather items are no longer crafted from tiger hide?**

   ____

4. **Find three images of Indian handicrafts and sketch them in the boxes below. Label the item and list the main material each is made from. Add colour.**

Paintings and murals

Use the 16 words from the box to complete the text about Indian murals.

cow	ceilings	create	murals	lighting	bacteria	busy	fat
animals	carved	hay	glue	tourists	century	outlines	chisel

The oldest paintings discovered in India are cave or rock paintings. These 1. _______________ were created using colours derived from natural materials mixed with animal 2. _______________, and show figures of humans and 3. _______________ in hunting and family scenes.

In 1819, in Maharashtra, India, John Smith, a British officer, discovered a series of exquisitely 4. _______________ caves while hunting for tigers. Dominating the walls, 5. _______________ and pillars of the 29 Ajanta caves are murals, which are considered as masterpieces by some. The paintings show different scenes from the life of Buddha, along with 6. _______________ scenes of everyday life.

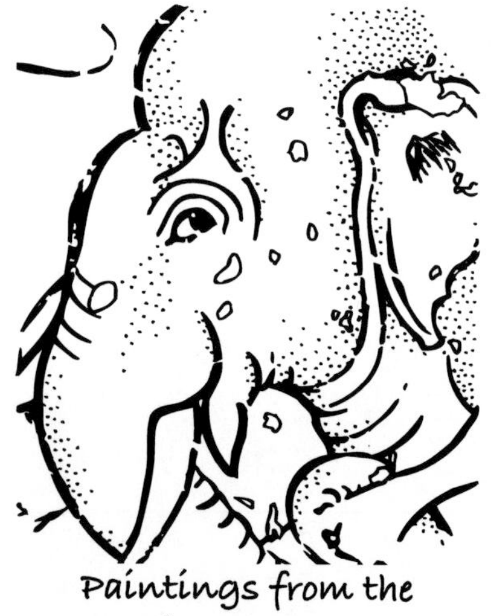

The Ajanta Caves

Some of the rock murals inside the caves date back to the second 7. _______________ BCE. The process of creating them involved a number of steps. First, the rock wall was 'roughened up' with a hammer and 8. _______________. Next, two coats of mud plaster (a mixture of clay, 9. _______________ or straw, animal hair and 10. _______________ dung) were applied followed by a thin coat of dried lime. While the plaster was still wet, several painters drew 11. _______________ from scenes and, finally, colour was applied which soaked into the plaster.

Some murals have sadly deteriorated due to a number of possible factors. The animal-derived 12. _______________ and vegetable gum used to 13. _______________ the colours was attractive to feeding insects and 14. _______________. Also, bat droppings combined with the humid breaths of the ever-increasing tourists have caused deterioration. Today, only small groups of 15. _______________ can enter the caves at one time, and 16. _______________ is kept to a minimum.

Paintings from the Ajanta Caves

Painting appreciation

1. (a) Choose a painting or mural by an Indian artist, showing a scene of India.

    (b) What are your **very first impressions** of the painting? Write notes in the box.

2. Now complete the following facts about the painting.

- My painting is called ________________________________ .

- The year it was painted was ________________________________ .

- The artist is ________________________________ .

- The paint medium is ________________________________ .

3. Complete the following about the painting.

(a) Describe what is happening in the painting.

(b) What does it tell you about life in India and Indian culture?

(c) What do you think the artist is trying to express in the painting?

(d) What do you like or dislike about the painting?

(e) How does the painting make you feel?

Music and dance .... page 89

Objective

Reads and completes information about the music and dance of India.

Teacher information

- The Gupta Empire, which lasted from early 4th to mid-6th century CE, was a time of great advances in the arts. During this period of India's history—called the 'Golden Period'—Indian classical music and dance were developed.

- Depending on the ability level of the class, a discussion may be required before pupils attempt Question 4. Discussion points could include:
  - What does the traditional music of your country sound like?
  - What are the main cultural aspects of your country?
  - Where does the majority of today's popular music come from? (USA, UK etc.)

Answers

1. (a) cymbals — solid   (b) flute — wind   (c) sitar — stringed   (d) drums — percussion;

2. (a) False   (b) True   (c) False

3. Classical dance originated in the temples, where it was used to illustrate Hindu mythology.

4. Answers will vary.

Additional activities

- Locate and sort the musical instruments in your school into the four categories: solid, wind, stringed, percussion

- What does a mandolin look like? How it is played? Use the Internet/resource centre to find out.

- Watch examples of Indian classical and folk dancing on the website 'Youtube™' (www.youtube.com).

Music and dance

Music in India is a traditional art form which has developed over thousands of years. It is an important expression of Indian culture. Indian music is performed in three forms—**vocal music**, **instrumental music** and **dance**. There are many different styles due to the vast number of ethnic groups in the country.

Early forms of vocal music were sacred hymns and chants sung using only one note. Gradually, this increased to using two, then seven notes. Vocal music can be performed by one or more singers and is sometimes accompanied by instruments.

There are many forms of classical and folk dances which vary from one region to the next. A wide variety of costumes are worn when performing them. Classical dance originated in the temples, where it was used to illustrate Hindu mythology.

The graceful dancer uses her body, limbs, hands, face and eyes to express her ideas or communicate a story, an idea or an emotion. Folk dances are usually simple, lively, joyful dances performed for special occasions.

Each region of India has its own folk or tribal dance, resulting in hundreds of different dances.

Indian musicians lead the field in instrumental music. There are as many as 500 instruments with different names which are played in a variety of ways. Instruments can be classified as: **solid** such as gongs and cymbals; **percussion** such as the drum; **wind** such as the organ, clarinet and flute; and **stringed** instruments such as the sitar and mandolin.

---

1. List the name and classification of each Indian musical instrument.

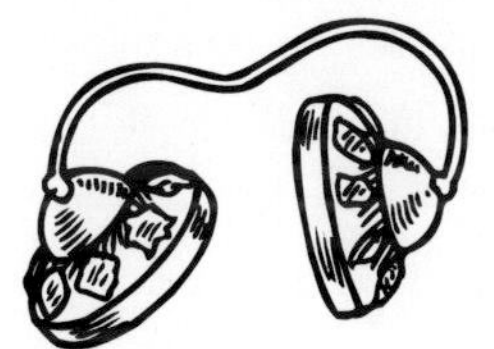   

(a) _____________   (b) _____________   (c) _____________   (d) _____________

_____________   _____________   _____________   _____________

2. Choose if each sentence is true or false.

(a) The same styles of music and dance can be found across India.   *True*   *False*

(b) Vocal music began as a form of worship.   *True*   *False*

(c) The main types of dancing are folk, classical and instrumental.   *True*   *False*

3. Where did Indian classical dance originate?

____

4. 'Indian music is an important expression of Indian culture.'

On the back of this sheet, explain if the same is true for music in your country.

Puppets and puppetry .... page 91

Objective

Reads and uses information to plan and write a play script.

Teacher information

- Puppets were (and are still) used in India, particularly in the rural areas, as a source of information and communication between people and, sometimes, government authorities. Traditionally, nomadic puppeteers shared any information they gathered in their travels by including it in their puppet scripts. Very importantly, puppets also provided a means of sharing and preserving the traditional stories of India. Many of these stories concerned the epics of the *Ramayana* and *Mahabharata*. Puppeteers ensured that these culturally-important stories were shared across many generations. This oral tradition meant that there were many versions of these stories.

- There were significant differences between the puppets used, and the stories and the characters they portrayed in one area of India from those in others areas. These differences reflected the diverse cultures of India.

- Pupils may prefer to work with a partner or in a small group to plan and write a play script. Their choice of characters and the qualities and values they reflect are important factors. They will also need to determine the problem confronting their characters and how they overcome it.

- Play scripts should be written on a separate page or computer. It is important that pupils are familiar with the conventions of writing a script and that they, for example, always identify the speaker.

- Remind pupils that plays are often introduced by a narrator. Discuss this role and explain how they are sometimes used to provide information about the setting and the characters, and to explain things the audience needs to know that may not be obvious.

Answers

Teacher check

Additional activities

- Use cardboard or paper to make flat puppet shapes glued on craft sticks. Use two torches to direct light from behind the puppets to demonstrate how their shadows can be seen from the front through a white cloth screen.

- Make a papier-mâché Indian animal puppet by shaping the head and neck with plasticine, then covering it with layers of small bits of paper and glue. When dry, cut the papier-mâché, remove the plasticine and paper over the join. When dry, paint the animals head. Cut a hole in a folded rectangular piece of fabric, place the head at the hole and attach the head to the fabric using elastic bands. The animal puppets could be used to tell an animal story.

Puppets and puppetry

Puppets have been described as **dolls that come alive**. Although they are found in countries around the world, many people believe puppets originated in India. This popular, traditional art form has been used in India for communication, education and entertainment since ancient times.

In India, a number of quite different types of puppets are used. These include:

- glove puppets, which are usually made of fabric with a wide skirt to go over the puppeteer's hand and arm. Three fingers, placed in the puppet's head and its two arms, make it move

- rod puppets, which are moved by wooden rods. These are attached to the puppet's hands and there is also one concealed in its body

- shadow puppets, which are flat and are often made of animal skin. They are placed behind a white cloth screen and light is directed on them from behind. Cane sticks, which the audience may not be able to see, are attached to the puppet. They are used to make the puppet move

- string puppets, which may have strings attached to many parts of their bodies. These puppets can move in lots of different ways but the puppeteer requires skill and practice to manipulate stings attached to two pieces of wood.

Puppets usually had a big head with large prominent eyes, no legs, and trailing skirts or robes. The males often wore a turban. They were very active and did a lot of fighting. The females had braided hair and held onto their skirts or saris as they danced around. Royal characters wore light-coloured clothes and had big moustaches. Villains were dark and had strange looking eyes.

Traditionally, puppeteers travelled around the country attending religious festivals and celebrations. Their shows were often managed by a family. The men manipulated the puppet strings and the females performed the music, singing and dialogue. Younger family members played the cymbals and the mridangam (drum). Stories told through the puppets were usually about good versus bad, winners versus losers, heroes versus cowards and generosity versus meanness.

1. **Plan, then write, a puppet play with four characters, set in India, Name your characters and briefly describe them using dot points.**

Character 1	Character 2	Character 3	Character 4

2. **What is the problem confronting your characters?**

3. **How do they solve the problem and what happens in the end?**

4. **Is there a moral message in this play? Explain.**

The Bollywood phenomenon .... page 93

Objective

Reads and comprehends information about the 'Bollywood' film industry of India.

Teacher information

- The term 'Bollywood' is frequently used to refer to the entire Indian film industry, but only incorporates the industry centred in Mumbai.

- Bollywood films are largely financed by private distributors or a few large studios. The industry has preferred producing films to appeal to all sections of a mainly urban Indian audience and, generally have not included narrower target audiences to maximise box office takings. However, this appears to be changing with films in the pipeline to cater for more rural Indian and overseas audiences.

- Bollywood employs people from all over India, although many of them are closely related to particular families in the Indian film industry. Very few non-Indian actors become stars in Bollywood. A large number of foreign extras are employed, however, as many Bollywood films are shot overseas or have sequences shot overseas. This last point has proved a winner in box office takings, so crews are increasingly travelling to film in United States, Canada, Australia, New Zealand and other countries.

- It is interesting to note that Bollywood film stars earn approximately two million dollars a film, but if they were in Hollywood they might make between six to 10 million dollars per film.

- Watching films in India is an extremely popular pastime. Touring cinemas travel to rural areas and set up a screen inside a massive tent. A thousand or more people might come to watch a film, some walking up to 15 kilometres to view it. (There are about 13 000 actual cinemas throughout India.)

Answers

1. (a) name   (b) American   (c) industry   (d) world   (e) three
   (f) film   (g) business   (h) happy   (i) seldom   (j) words
   (k) Indian   (l) female   (m) audience   (n) Bollywood   (o) fans
   (p) before

Additional activity

- Pupils could view a suitable Bollywood film(s) and write a review about it/them considering the following points: type of plot (melodramatic, romantic etc.), roles played by main and minor characters, acting performances, actors singing and dancing performance (if appropriate), costumes, set design, lighting, sound quality, set locations (in India or overseas) and individual pupil's opinions of the film.

The Bollywood phenomenon

Choose words from the box below to complete the text about the Bollywood phenomenon.

happy	*audience*	*before*	*seldom*	*name*	*words*	
American	*film*	*industry*	*female*	*Bollywood*		
business	*three*	*fans*	*world*	*Indian*		

'Bollywood' is the name given to the Indian film industry—it is not an actual physical location. It gets this (a) _______________ from combining 'Hollywood', the centre of the (b) _______________ film industry, with 'Bombay', the former name for Mumbai and centre of the Hindi-language film (c) _______________.

Bollywood has been the largest producer of films in the (d) _______________ since it overtook America in the 1970s. More than 1000 films are produced each year.

A typical Bollywood film is about (e) _______________ hours in length with an intermission part way through. The majority are musicals with catchy song-and-dance numbers. A film's music is often released before the (f) _______________, with the aim to increase box office takings. The plots are quite melodramatic, involving complicated love triangles, kidnappings, relatives separated by fate, corrupt (g) _______________ people and scheming villains. Added to this are unbelievable coincidences, big helpings of comedy and there is nearly always a (h) _______________ ending.

The sound on a Bollywood film is (i) _______________ recorded on location. The songs are prerecorded by professional playback singers. The actors lip-sync (mime the mouth movements) the (j) _______________ to the songs. Dances performed in a film are based on (k) _______________ classical dance styles or folk dances and often combined with Western-style dances. The male or (l) _______________ lead actor usually performs with a troupe of supporting dancers. The majority of film scripts and song lyrics are written in Hindustani, so the widest possible (m) _______________ understands it. However, Indian English is appearing more frequently.

Since the 2000s, (n) _______________ productions have grown in popularity, not just to adoring Indian (o) _______________ but to an increasing worldwide audience. One large problem facing Bollywood is copyright infringements, with pirated copies of films being released (p) _______________ the actual film.

Famous people

Objective

Reads information and completes a compare and contrast chart about Mahatma Gandhi and Indira Gandhi.

Teacher information

- The name 'Mahatma', meaning 'great soul', was used to describe Gandhi. He fought for the rights of people in South Africa and then in India, where the plight of the lowest class of Indian society, the 'untouchables', or as he called them harijans (meaning 'Children of God'), became his major concern. His amazing courage, persistence and success in solving social problems without resorting to violence were said to have inspired others, including Martin Luther King Jr and Nelson Mandela.

- His belief that political and social progress could best be achieved by nonviolent protests (such as the boycotting of British goods and institutions and acts of civil disobedience) led to thousands of arrests.

- One incident of civil disobedience occurred in 1930 after poor people were stopped from making their own salt. He led a 390 km protest march to Dandi Beach to break the law by gathering salt there.

- In 1942, he was involved in the Quit India movement. After a protest became violent, he was imprisoned. He was released two years later after the death of his wife, Kasturba (they had married when they were only 13), and because he was ill with malaria.

- Gandhi recognised that the lack of religious tolerance between the Muslims and Hindus was a serious impediment to independence and he was strongly opposed to the partitioning of the country. He worked to reconcile these differences and his assassination by a Hindu extremist was a consequence of his attempts to bring the Muslims and Hindus together. The extreme violence and loss of life after partition validated his concern about this issue.

- Gandhi was to have been awarded the Nobel Peace Prize in 1948. After his assassination, it was decided not to award a prize that year.

- Indira Gandhi was India's first female prime minister and when she became prime minister only its fifth. Politics and the struggle for independence had been part her life since early childhood. She was an only child. After her father became India's first prime minister, she was deeply involved in politics but didn't enter parliament until after his death. Shastri, the country's third prime minister, died in 1966 shortly after the war with Pakistan had been won, and (after a short term by an interim prime minister) she took over as prime minister. She was elected to that position the following year.

- As prime minister, she worked to improve agriculture and as a result of what was called the 'green revolution', India was able to export rice, wheat, cotton and milk. Technology and science were encouraged and India conducted underground nuclear tests in 1974 and sent its first satellite into space in 1971.

- Indira Gandhi had two sons: one was killed in a flying accident and the other became prime minister in 1984 and was assassinated five years later.

- A similarities-and-differences chart is a simple graphic organiser with two columns which allows pupils to compare and contrast information provided in a text. They need to select relevant facts for inclusions in their chart by making associations and finding connections. Dot points and brief sentences or phrases should be used to record this information.

Additional activities

- Make a comicstrip-style illustration showing the assassination of Indira Gandhi by her Sikh bodyguards in her home gardens and the events leading up to it.

- Write a letter to the man who demanded that Mahatma Gandhi be moved into a third class carriage. Pupils should be encouraged to explain their opinions of his actions and their consequences. They should try to persuade him to share these opinions.

Mahatma Gandhi and Indira Gandhi

Mahatma Gandhi

'Generations to come will scarce believe that such a man as this walked the earth in flesh and blood.'

What special kind of man was described this way, in 1948, by Albert Einstein, one of the most intelligent people to have ever lived?

This quiet, shy man, Mohandas Gandhi, known as the 'Father of the Nation', was born in India in 1869. With incredible courage and determination he led a peaceful revolution that over many years, changed the lives of millions of people around the world.

Gandhi was a lawyer who had studied in India and England before working for 20 years with a law firm in South Africa. His determination to fight for the rights of Indian people started after an incident in which he was thrown from a train on a cold night. He'd paid for a first class ticket so when a man objected to travelling with him, he refused to be relocated to a third class carriage. Soon after, he began speaking publicly about the need for political and social change and how this should be achieved through nonviolent protest. By 1914, the South African government had agreed to his proposed changes.

Back in India, Gandhi worked for years to secure India's independence from Britain. Although imprisoned on numerous occasions, he continued to make speeches encouraging nonviolent protest and civil disobedience. He was invited to England for negotiations in 1931, but was arrested on his return.

Gandhi later made a huge effort to improve the relationship between India's Hindus and Muslims. But sadly he couldn't prevent the many riots and deaths that occurred after India's independence. He was shot by a Hindu extremist in 1948.

Indira Gandhi

Indira Nehru was born in 1917 into a very influential and politically active family. Her father, Jawaharlal, became India's first prime minister at independence in 1947.

Indira's early life was dominated by the fight for Indian independence happening around her. Her father, like many of those working for independence, spent some time in prison. Even as a child she made her opinions known by protesting when police came to their home to remove furniture to pay for her father's prison fines. She once showed courage by smuggling secret plans for a revolution against the British out of the family's house in her school bag. At 12, as leader of the 'Monkey Brigade', she gave speeches and helped this group of children to warn people who were about to be arrested.

While studying at Oxford University in England she met Feroza Gandhi, the adopted son of Mahatma Gandhi, whom she married in 1942. He entered parliament and later became the editor of a national newspaper until his death in 1960. They had two sons, Sanjay and Rajiv. Indira was her father's chief of staff and also president of the Indian National Congress.

When her father died in 1964, Indira entered parliament and became the Minister of Information and Broadcasting. She became the fifth prime minister in 1966. She encouraged science and technology and worked to reduce poverty, establishing good relations with the Soviets and Chinese but not with the Americans.

In 1984, she was assassinated by her Sikh bodyguards after she had ordered troops to enter a Sikh sacred shrine, the Golden Temple, looking for terrorists. Her son Rajiv, who gave up his job as a pilot to enter politics, became prime minister in 1984 and was assassinated in 1991.

Complete a similarity-and-differences chart on a separate page using the information you have read about Mahatma Gandhi and Indira Gandhi.

Famous people

Mother Teresa: a woman of great love.......................................page 97

Objective

Reads information and completes an information chart about Mother Teresa.

Teacher information

- Mother Teresa, an Albanian, was born in Skopje in what is now Macedonia. After her father died when she was eight, life for her family was more difficult. When she was very young, she decided to devote her life to looking after the needy and left home to go to the Sisters of Loretto in Ireland when she was 18. After a short time there, she was sent to St Mary's School in Calcutta where she worked for about 20 years as a teacher and later as principal. Leaving the convent in 1948, she started an open-air school without any funds or assistance. But two years later she had gained sufficient support to establish her own order, the Missionaries of Charity. By 1957, this order had expanded beyond India and was working internationally with lepers and caring for people in many of the world's disaster areas. Missionaries of Charity became an International Religious Family by papal decree in 1965. At the time of her death in 1997, there were 4000 sisters working in 610 foundations in 123 different countries.

- A KWL chart is a useful graphic organiser which provides pupils with a framework for organising information from text, and their thoughts and ideas about it. Pupils should use dot points and brief sentences or phrases to enter information.

Additional activities

- Discuss possible reasons to explain why world leaders and some of the world's most famous and influential people went to visit Mother Teresa and why she encouraged the publicity and attention generated by these high profile visitors.

- Pupils write a similar report about someone they know, or know of, who puts the welfare and care of others before his or her own needs.

Mother Teresa: a woman of great love

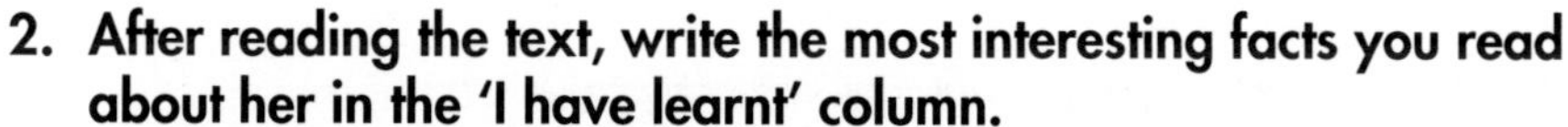

What do you know about Mother Teresa?

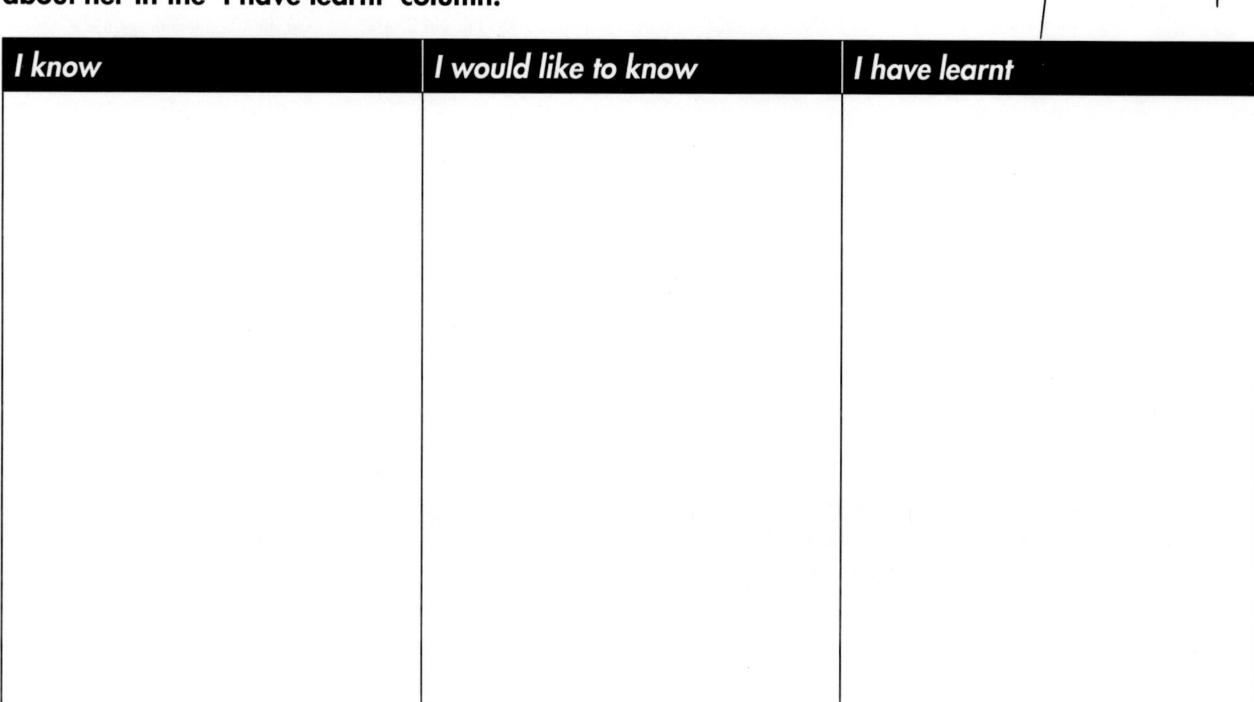

1. Before you read the text below:

(a) Write some facts you know about her in the 'I know' column of the chart.

(b) Think about what you would like to know about her and write two or three questions in the 'I would like to know' column of the chart.

2. After reading the text, write the most interesting facts you read about her in the 'I have learnt' column.

I know	I would like to know	I have learnt

After arriving in India from Europe in 1929 (when she was 19) and teaching at St Mary's High School, in Calcutta, Agnesë Bojaxhiu decided two years later to become a nun. She chose the name Teresa, the patron saint of missionaries.

The health and suffering of many of the poorest people living in Calcutta's slums concerned her so much that, in 1948, she asked the Pope for permission to live outside the nun's convent to take care of them. She then spent three months working at a hospital to learn about nursing. Over the next three years, she started a school for the poorest children, set up orphanages where street children could live and established a home for the dying and destitute. People of all religions were always welcomed and were given the same care and respect.

Mother Teresa became famous in 1969 after a film about her work and a book called Something beautiful for God *was published. Many other nuns soon came to join her Missionaries of Charity. With the help of volunteers and money donated from around the world, similar centres were established in 123 countries.*

Mother Teresa's life's work was recognised in many ways, including being awarded the Nobel Peace Prize in 1979 and the American Presidential Medal of Freedom in 1985. She died of heart failure in 1997.

Famous people

Abhinav Bindra .... page 99

Objective

Reads information and answers questions about Abhinav Bindra.

Teacher information

- Abhinav was born in Zirakpur, India in September 1982. His family had the finances needed to develop his shooting abilities and when he was 13, they took him to meet Col. Jagir Singh Dhillon, a local shooting coach. By the time he was 15, he had qualified to shoot in the 1998 Kuala Lumpur Commonwealth Games.

- After the joy of breaking the world record and the disappointment of not winning a medal at the Athens Olympics, Abhinav was immobilised with severe back pain. There were doubts whether he would be able to continue shooting. But despite the pain, he continued and was the only Indian in the finals of the World Cup in Milan in 2001. He was placed sixth. In 2002, he was awarded India's highest sporting honour, the Rajiv Gandhi Khel Rahna award. In 2006, He became the first Indian shooter to win the World Cup.

- After he achieved his historic gold medal in Beijing, Abhinav was well rewarded with cash prizes and government grants, including a lifetime gold pass from India Railways. During his speaking tours around the country, he promotes the sport of shooting which is not considered by some to be a spectator sport.

Answers

1. (a) 1980   (b) the men's hockey team

2. Possible answers include: They were probably rich because they could provide his equipment and build him a shooting range and they could send him overseas to study.

3. It is likely that Abhinav can speak English because he would need to speak it to study in America.

4. Possible factors include: parental encouragement, good trainers, equipment and facilities, talent, interest, determination, good concentration, a steady hand, good eyesight

5. Possible answers include lack of: money, community interest, publicity, coaches, training resources, government support, business sponsorship and the strong interest in team sports such as cricket and hockey.

Additional activities

- Write three facts and three opinions about Abhinav Bindra.

- Write a newspaper article suitable for an Indian newspaper telling about Abhinav's win at the Beijing Olympics in August 2008.
  Remember to:

  - choose an attention-grabbing headline

  - make it look like a newspaper article by writing in columns and adding an illustration

  - make it sound exciting because it was a very special occasion in India.

Abhinav Bindra

The date 11 August 2008 marked an important event in India—it was the day India won its first ever individual Olympic gold medal. Before that day, it had always been a win in cricket that caused the greatest excitement around the country. But this changed dramatically for one very special day when a young Indian man, Abhinav Bindra, won gold in the 10-metre air rifle competition in Beijing. It was even more exciting because it had been a very long 28 years since India had seen any Olympic gold at all: a team medal in men's hockey.

Four years earlier, it had been very disappointing. At the previous Olympics in Athens, Abhinav broke the Olympic record, for shooting, but he then failed to go on and win an Olympic medal.

Abhinav was a successful international competitor at a young age, having been the youngest competitor (15 years old) at the Commonwealth Games in 1998. In 2002 Commonwealth Games, he won gold in the pairs and an individual silver. He even won the World Championship in 2006. But his accomplishment in 2008 was different—it was an Olympic gold medal!

He was a hero! The rewards and recognition that came his way were amazing. Now, as a national hero, he spends a lot of time travelling around the country giving speeches and talking about his achievements. One of the things he often speaks about is the need for the Indian government and private businesses to encourage and support sports in India other than cricket.

Abhinav has a commerce degree from the University of Colorado in the United States and now runs his own business. For many years he was supported and encouraged to shoot by his parents. He has always had the very best equipment and facilities and has been trained by some of the world's best coaches at an indoor shooting range his parents had built for him at their home.

1. (a) In which year was India's previous Olympic gold medal won? _______________

   (b) Who won it? ____

2. **You could conclude that Abhinav's parents were** _________________________ **(rich/poor)**

   because ____

   ____

3. (a) Do you think Abhinav can speak English? _____________________________

   (b) Explain why you think this. _____________________________________

   ____

4. **List some of the factors that could have contributed to Abhinav's success.**

   ____

   ____

5. **Explain why you think India hasn't won many individual Olympic medals.**

   ____

   ____

Famous people

Objective

Reads information and answers questions about Aishwarya Rai.

Teacher information

- Aishwarya Rai was born in 1973. Her traditional Indian family lived in the south. She is an intelligent, well educated, charming and hugely popular film star in India and has also achieved international success.

- While an architecture student, she began part-time modelling and appeared in advertisements for some very popular products. Despite many requests, she refused offers to model full-time so she could concentrate on her studies. But this all changed after she was chosen as Miss World because she became even better known in India and overseas and many more modelling opportunities were available to her. Then film offers came pouring in.

- She was already a very well established film star in India before she accepted offers from overseas. *Bride and prejudice* was her first English-speaking role. She was only the sixth Indian to feature in London's Madame Tussaud's wax museum and the first Indian woman.

- Aishwarya married in a traditional Hindu ceremony in 2007. She continues her film career and works for charity.

Answers

1. (a) false   (b) false   (c) false

2. Possible answers include: She was a successful model who people saw in magazines and advertisements. There would have been lots of publicity when an Indian woman was crowned Miss World.

3. Possible answers include: People around the world knew about her and she became even better known in India. People everywhere wanted to see the world's most beautiful woman. Indians felt proud of her.

4. Possible answers include: Hollywood is the centre of the very big and successful American film industry. They tried to make a connection between Hollywood and the very big and highly successful Indian film industry by calling it Bollywood. The same kind of things happen in both places.

Additional activities

- Write a similar description about a film star you admire.

- If you were a successful film star, which charity would you like to support? Explain your reasons for choosing this charity.

Aishwarya Rai

India and its culture were showcased in a most spectacular way at the closing ceremony of the 2006 Commonwealth Games in Melbourne. This was done to promote the 2010 Delhi Commonwealth Games to the thousands of people at the ceremony and to the worldwide television audience.

Probably the most famous person taking part in this promotion was the very beautiful Indian actress, Aishwarya Rai. A former top model and film star, she has acted in more than 40 films produced in both India and Hollywood. She is a very familiar face to millions of Indians and is also known to many overseas film fans. This Indian film star is often referred to as the 'Queen of Bollywood'.

Aishwarya Rai, who was runner up in the Miss India contest, won the title of Miss World in 1994. After 12 months of travelling the world in this role, she returned to modelling. She appeared on the cover of world famous fashion magazines and in advertisements for different products, including a popular soft drink distributed internationally. In India, her face was already a very familiar one before she began her highly successful career as a film star.

Devdas, a 2002 film starring Aishwarya Rai, is considered the most successful film in Bollywood's history. It was given a special screening at the Cannes Film Festival, then broke box office records in India and the United States (as the highest grossing Indian film).

Hollywood films in which Aishwarya Rai has starred include, Bride and prejudice (2003) and The pink panther 2 (2009). She is very much in demand because of her beauty, her talent and because she speaks four languages: Hindi, Tamil, Urdu and English.

Underprivileged girls in India and the victims of disasters like the 2004 Boxing Day tsunami are the focus of Aishwarya's continuing charity work.

---

1. Choose if each sentence is true or false.

    (a) Aishwarya Rai was crowned Miss India.   **True   False**

    (b) Aishwarya was at the opening of the 2006 Commonwealth Games.   **True   False**

    (c) The name 'Queen of Bollywood' was given to Aishwarya because she went to Hollywood to star in a film.   **True   False**

2. Why did people know who Aishwarya was before she acted in films?

____

____

3. How would being Miss World have helped Aishwarya's career?

____

____

4. Why do you think the Indian film industry is called 'Bollywood'?

____

____